BEER
SNACKS

TASTY BITES FROM AROUND THE WORLD

BEER SNACKS

Oscar Smith

Smith
Street
Books

Introduction page 6

Contents

DIPS

PLATES

BASICS

Introduction

Beer and snacks, together forever. It is often said that in the most successful relationships, partners bring out the best in each other. If so, can you think of a better pairing? Drinking beer without snacks can leave you hungry, tired and frankly, too drunk. And snacks without beer? Who would even bother?

It's a sacred relationship that is embraced and honoured the world over, and one of the best elements of travel is discovering all of the new and delicious ways in which this combo can occur. This book explores the best beer snacks from all over the globe, from nibbles to share with a pre-dinner libation, through to heartier fare for those settling in to a session.

Before you snack...
a quick guide to beer

There are so many different styles of beer to keep up with, especially with the popularity of craft beer exploding worldwide. Beer styles can vary wildly, from bitter, floral hoppiness to sweet, biscuity maltiness; from high-alcohol sippers to low-alcohol sessionable ales; big, dark, smoky beers to light, crisp, clear ones – as well as everything in between. To help you pick the perfect beer for your snack, here's a basic overview of some of the major beer categories.

LAGER

Lager is the term for beer that is fermented at a lower temperature. They're often quite clear, crisp and lightly hopped. There should be some bitterness in the drink from the hops, without being overpoweringly bitter. There are plenty of good lagers in the world, but unfortunately, there are more terrible ones – often sold in tall, see-through bottles.

DARK LAGER

This is beer that is cold-fermented, but using toasted, darker malts. This process imparts colour and flavour into the beer. Dark lagers can range from caramelly, full-bodied amber beers, all the way through to smoky, chocolatey black beers.

PALE ALE

'Pale ale' can technically mean many different things. While it sounds like it's referring just to the appearance of the beer, generally speaking, if you see 'pale ale' on a beer label these days, it means it has been made in the American style, with up-front floral fruitiness and a light bitterness on the finish. Despite the name, pale ales can sometimes be quite amber in colour.

IPA

'India pale ale' is not from India. It was created in England to last the long voyage at sea to get to India. It was made with higher alcohol and a shirt-load of hops to act as a preservative. It is very bitter and probably not great for a first-time beer drinker, but it's very rewarding once you've acquired the taste.

SAISON

Saison is a style of beer created by the Belgians. Traditionally, it was a low-alcohol farmhouse ale made for the workers using all the leftover grains and hops from the proper brew. As with most old-fashioned peasant food, it has been perfected over the years, and is now one of the most versatile beer styles around. Because of the mish-mash of ingredients, the flavours of saison can vary substantially and the opportunities for brewers to interpret the style are almost endless. Experiment with different ones to find your favourite.

WHEAT BEER

Wheat beer is made from – you guessed it – wheat, instead of barley. Pale in colour, and often lower in alcohol, wheat beer has a distinct mouthfeel and a light, fruity flavour. Sometimes wheat beer is flavoured with cloves, orange rind or even coriander (cilantro). There are many different names for wheat beer: witbier, hefeweizen and weissbier are all different words for different styles. Weizen is German for 'wheat', and hefe means 'yeast'. Therefore, hefeweizen is a wheat beer that has been bottle-conditioned and contains some yeast sediment. The Germans also have kristallweizen, which is a clear wheat beer and dunkelweizen which is a dark wheat beer. There is also witbier or weissbier which translates to 'white beer'. These are your standard wheat beers from the Netherlands, Belgium and Germany. The French call it bière blanche.

BROWN ALE

Brown ales are usually more malt-driven than pale ales. This lends the beer nutty, caramelly characteristics, with less bitterness and more sweetness.

PORTER

This is a black beer made from dark, toasted malt, but usually without the burnt bitterness of a stout. Porters can often be quite sweet, with rich flavours of coffee and chocolate.

STOUT

Similar to porter, but generally not as sweet, stouts can vary greatly in style. Irish stout, such as Guinness, tends to be gassed with nitrogen instead of carbon dioxide, resulting in a beer with smaller bubbles and a creamy head. Milk stout has lactose sugar added, to impart a sweet caramel flavour. Oatmeal stout has a smooth mouthfeel and a lingering sweetness.

BELGIAN ALES

The Belgians are the masters of brewing. The Trappist monks have been doing it for a thousand years. Belgian ales range in style from lighter, malty blonde ales, all the way to high-alcohol dark ales. Belgian beers are very traditional and stay true to their style, so you won't find a lot of up-front floral hoppiness as you do with some modern beers.

SOURS & LAMBICS

These styles are really having their moment in the sun right now with a huge range of sours, especially, being produced by fun-loving craft brewers all over the world. Sour beers often use wild yeast and open-vat fermentation, creating very unusual flavours that sometimes make you question whether you're drinking a beer at all. You will often find sour beers flavoured with fruit such as raspberries, strawberries, guava and watermelon.

Chicharrones

SERVES

4–6

500 g (1 lb 2 oz) pork skin, or pork
crackling, scored and cut into
3 cm (1¼ in) wide strips
1 tablespoon sea salt flakes
2 teaspoons chilli powder
vegetable oil, for deep-frying

Preheat the oven to 150°C (300°F).

Place the cut strips of pork skin, fat side down, on a wire rack set over a roasting tin (to catch the melting fat). Transfer to the oven and bake for 1 hour.

Reduce the oven temperature to 120°C (250°F), or as low as it will go, and bake for a further 1½ hours to dry the pork skin out.

In a small bowl, combine the salt and chilli powder. Set aside.

In a large saucepan or deep-fryer, heat the oil to 180°C (350°F). Carefully fry the pork strips a few at a time, taking care as the hot oil may spit. Cook for 45–60 seconds, or until the pork strips puff up and are golden brown in colour.

Remove with a slotted spoon to a wire rack and dust with the chilli salt.

Serve immediately, or store in a clean airtight container in the pantry for up to 4 days.

While you can snack on pork rinds in fine drinking establishments the world over, nothing comes close to a plate of spicy chicharrón in Mexico City. Salud!

Honey caramel, bacon & macadamia popcorn

SERVES

8–10

2 tablespoons olive oil

125 g (4½ oz) rindless loin (back) bacon, diced

75 g (2¾ oz/⅓ cup) popping corn

3 tablespoons honey

150 g (5½ oz/⅔ cup) caster (superfine) sugar

125 g (4½ oz/½ cup) unsalted butter, chopped

100 g (3½ oz/¾ cup) salted macadamia nuts, roughly chopped

Heat 2 teaspoons of the oil in a frying pan over medium-high heat and cook the bacon for 6–8 minutes, or until very well browned and crisp. Remove with a slotted spoon and drain on paper towel.

Pour the bacon fat from the pan, plus the remaining olive oil, into a large heavy-based saucepan and place over medium heat. After a minute or so, test to see if the oil mixture is hot enough by adding a couple of corn kernels to the pan – they should spin slowly. Add the corn, shake the pan to coat in the oil mixture and cover with a lid. Shake the pan regularly until the popping ceases. Remove from the heat and tip the popped corn into a large heatproof bowl. Discard any unpopped corn and set the bowl aside.

Stir the honey, sugar and butter in a heavy-based saucepan over low heat until the sugar dissolves. Increase the heat to medium and boil for 4–5 minutes without stirring, or until you have a golden brown caramel.

Remove from the heat, stir in the macadamia nuts and bacon, then pour the mixture over the popped corn. Working quickly, gently fold the mixture until the corn is well combined (a silicon spatula is really useful for this task). Spread the mixture over a baking paper-lined tray and set aside for 30 minutes or until cool and set. Break into pieces to serve.

Store in an airtight container in the fridge for 3–4 days (if there's any left by then).

This popcorn is also great made with roasted salted peanuts instead of macadamia nuts.

Lemon & thyme marinated olives

4–6

250 ml (8 fl oz/1 cup) olive oil

peel from 1 lemon, any pith removed

3 garlic cloves, peeled and halved lengthways

4–5 fresh thyme sprigs

3 thin slices lemon, each cut into 6 wedges

300 g (10½ oz) assorted olives

Pour the oil into a small saucepan over low heat and add the lemon peel, garlic and thyme. Cook for 2–3 minutes – the garlic and lemon peel will fizz gently, but should not change colour.

Remove from the heat, leave to cool for 5 minutes, then add the lemon slices and olives and toss to combine. Pour into a sterilised jar and leave for 2–3 hours for the flavours to infuse before serving.

The olives will keep, in the fridge, for 1–2 weeks. The olives should be submerged in the oil – if they are not, just top up with a more olive oil. Give the jar a good few turns before opening and serving.

Olives with chorizo, capsicum and almonds

Add 50 g (1¾ oz/⅓ cup) blanched almonds to the olive oil and heat and cool in a small saucepan as above. When adding the olives, also add one chopped marinated red capsicum (bell pepper) and one cooked spicy chorizo sausage, cut into small cubes.

Olives with feta

Make the olives as described above, but omit the thyme and add one finely diced long red chilli to the oil. Add 100 g (3½ oz) Greek feta cut into small cubes and ½ teaspoon dried oregano with the olives.

Pickle chips

SERVES

4–6

125 ml (4 fl oz/½ cup) whole
  buttermilk
1 teaspoon freshly ground black
  pepper
450 g (16 oz) dill pickle slices,
  drained
225 g (8 oz/1½ cups) cornmeal
75 g (2¾ oz/½ cup) plain
  (all-purpose) flour
canola oil, for deep-frying
hot sauce, to serve

Line a baking tray with baking paper.

Combine the buttermilk and pepper in a shallow bowl.
Add the pickles and stir to coat.

Combine the cornmeal and flour in another shallow dish.
Add several pickles at a time, and toss to coat evenly in
the cornmeal mixture. Place on the baking tray.

Heat the oil in a saucepan or deep-fryer to 180°C (350°F).
Add the pickles, in batches, and fry for 1–2 minutes until
golden brown and crisp. Drain on paper towel, sprinkle
with salt and serve drenched in your favourite hot sauce.

You'll find pickle chips in the best dive bars in the American South. Drench with hot sauce and wash them down with a Bud Light.

A Malaysian classic, you'll find variations on ikan bilis throughout Southeast Asia. Dried anchovies fried with peanuts make for a bowlful of crunchy salty goodness.

Ikan bilis

SERVES

4

100 g (3½ oz/⅔ cup) raw peanuts
1 long red chilli, roughly chopped
2 garlic cloves
2 teaspoons grated ginger
100 g (3½ oz) dried anchovies
vegetable oil

Preheat the oven to 180°C (350°F).

Spread the peanuts on a baking tray, then toast them in the oven for about 10 minutes, until lightly golden.

Using a mortar and pestle, grind the chilli, garlic and ginger to a paste, then set aside.

Rinse the anchovies well in cold water, drain, pat dry, then leave to dry on paper towel.

Heat enough oil for deep-frying in a saucepan or deep-fryer to 160°C (320°F). Fry the anchovies in two batches, each for 3–4 minutes, until crispy. The anchovies will continue to cook once out of the oil, so remove them from the pan before they are fully cooked. Leave to drain on paper towel.

Heat the 1 tablespoon of oil in a frying pan over medium heat and cook the paste for 2–3 minutes, until fragrant. Add the peanuts and anchovies, stir to coat in the paste, then remove from the heat. Leave to cool, then serve. Store in an airtight container.

BEER

SNACKS

Miso edamame

SERVES

4

320 g (11½ oz) edamame, in their
  pods, fresh or frozen
2 tablespoons red miso paste
1 teaspoon sugar
1 tablespoon mirin
2 teaspoons sesame seeds,
  toasted

For fresh edamame, cook the edamame in boiling water for 5–6 minutes. For frozen, cook according to the packet instructions. Drain.

Heat a wok over high heat, then add the miso paste, sugar, mirin and 80 ml (2½ fl oz/⅓ cup) water. Mix well, bring to the boil, then add the edamame. Reduce the heat and cook for 2–3 minutes, until the water has reduced and the sauce is coating the edamame.

Add the sesame seeds, give everything a final stir and serve hot, with a spare bowl for the discarded pods.

Edamame with chilli–lime salt

Combine 2 tablespoons sea salt flakes, 1 teaspoon chilli flakes and the zest of 1 lime in a mortar. Use the pestle to grind the mixture until the salt flakes are broken down and everything is well mixed. Boil the edamame as described above and serve the salt in a ramekin alongside, for dipping.

Sriracha edamame

Mix 4 tablespoons sriracha sauce with 20 g (¾ oz) melted butter until well combined. Boil the edamame as described above, toss in the sauce and serve.

A massive pile of edamame next to a huge, frosty pint of Asahi Black is one of the finest views you'll find in Japan.

BIA HOI !!!
BIA HOI !!!
BIA HOI !!!
BIA HOI !!!
BIA HOI !!!

Bia Hoi Hanoi

The best way to cope with the hustle of Hanoi's hectic streets is to just succumb to it. And the best way to do that is to pull up a tiny blue stool on a street corner in the Old Quarter and enjoy a glass – or ten – of the city's fresh draught beer, Bia Hoi Hanoi.

Fresh beer

Bia hoi means 'fresh beer' (the beer is brewed daily and is meant to be consumed within 24 hours of production), and it refers both to the beverage and the establishment in which it's enjoyed. In Hanoi, bia hois range from a hole in the wall with plastic furniture spilling onto the street, to huge fluoro-lit halls pouring out keg after keg to thirsty locals. Refrigeration is generally eschewed, with kegs being chilled by enormous bricks of ice.

It's some of the cheapest beer in the world and tends towards a low alcohol volume, meaning you can easily down glass after glass in order to chase away the heat. Cheers those at neighbouring tables with a rousing cry of 'môt, hai, ba, vô!'

Fresh food

Sit at a bia hoi long enough and you'll be offered an array of snacks from passing vendors: mysterious banana-leaf parcels (usually containing steamed ground pork); raw peanuts in their shells; huge puffy rice crackers covered in seeds or dried shrimp; popcorn (also containing dried shrimp); and a few Western imports that have become local obsessions – fries and deep-fried mozzarella sticks.

If your bia hoi serves food, you're in for a treat. Look for deep-fried pork spring rolls or fried tofu (usually made that day), both served with mountains of fresh herbs.

Mixed fruit with chilli salt

SERVES

10–12

3 tablespoons sea salt flakes
2 teaspoons chilli flakes
1 pineapple
¼ large wedge of watermelon,
    about 800 g–1 kg
    (1 lb 12 oz–2 lb 3 oz)
2 oranges
1 telegraph (long) cucumber

Combine the salt and chilli flakes in a mortar, then use the pestle to grind them until the salt flakes break down and the salt is well mixed. Place in a small serving bowl.

Peel and core the pineapple, cut it into 1 cm (½ in) slices and then into wedges. Slice the watermelon into wedges. Cut each orange into eight wedges. Cut the cucumber into thirds lengthways, then slice each length into four to six batons.

Arrange the fruit on a platter and serve with the bowl of chilli salt for dipping.

Fruit, chilli and salt is a classic combo common throughout much of Asia, especially in the south. A little bit sweet, a little bit salty and a little bit spicy – this snack has it all.

Boiled salted peanuts

SERVES

6–8

500 g (1 lb 2 oz) raw (green) peanuts in their shells
90 g (3 oz) salt
hot sauce, to serve

Rinse the peanuts under cold water, then place them in a large saucepan. Cover with water, add the salt and bring to the boil over high heat.

Cover the pan, reduce the heat and leave to simmer for about 3 hours. Check occasionally, adding more water as needed when it gets low.

Test after 3 hours – the nuts should be soft and slightly salty. If the peanuts aren't salty enough for your liking, add another 20 g ($\frac{3}{4}$ oz) salt and simmer for another 15 minutes.

Leave the peanuts to cool slightly in the water, then drain and serve warm, covered in your favourite hot sauce. The cooled peanuts will keep in the fridge for 5–7 days.

Variation

Add 2 tablespoons of seasoning, such as Old Bay Seasoning, Cajun spice mix, stock powder or smoked paprika, to the water along with the salt.

Boiled peanuts are iconic to the American South and also known, depending on your aspect, as either 'redneck edamame' or 'the caviar of the South'.

Mixed pickled vegetables

SERVES
8–10

3–4 baby cucumbers

4 baby carrots

1 small red capsicum (bell pepper)

1 small yellow capsicum
(bell pepper)

4–5 baby eggplants (aubergines)

10–12 button mushrooms

¼ head cauliflower

8–10 cherry tomatoes

2–4 bay leaves

2 garlic cloves, sliced

½ teaspoon black peppercorns

935 ml (31½ fl oz/3¾ cups) white
vinegar

3 tablespoons sugar

3 teaspoons salt

Clean and sterilise two 1 litre (34 fl oz) mason or other heatproof jars.

Cut the ends off the cucumbers, then slice the cucumbers into four pieces. Wash and peel the carrots, then slice them into thick batons, depending on their thickness. Remove the core and seeds of the capsicums and cut into thick batons. Place the cucumber, carrot and capsicum into one of the jars.

Halve or quarter the eggplants, depending on their size. Cut any larger mushrooms in half. Cut the cauliflower into small florets. Place the eggplant, mushrooms, cauliflower and cherry tomatoes in the second jar.

Divide the bay leaves, garlic cloves and peppercorns between the jars.

Put the vinegar, 750 ml (25½ fl oz/3 cups) water, the sugar and salt in a saucepan and bring to the boil. Lower the heat and simmer for 2–3 minutes, stirring to make sure the sugar and salt have dissolved. Remove from the heat, leave to cool for 3–4 minutes, then pour the liquid over the vegetables in the jars until they are covered (you may not need all the liquid). Leave to cool, then cover and transfer to the refrigerator. Leave to pickle for at least 2–3 days before serving. The pickles will keep for up to 1 month in the refrigerator.

Sesame & chilli lotus root chips

SERVES

4–6

½ teaspoon salt

1 teaspoon black sesame seeds, toasted

1 teaspoon white sesame seeds, toasted

1 teaspoon gochugaru (Korean chilli powder) (see note)

200 g (7 oz) lotus root, scrubbed

dash of vinegar or lemon juice, if necessary

vegetable oil, for deep-frying

Mix together the salt, black and white sesame seeds and gochugaru in a bowl and set aside.

Peel the lotus root, then use a sharp knife or mandoline to cut it into very thin slices – around 1 mm ($\frac{1}{16}$ in) thick.

Lay the slices on paper towel and pat dry. Lotus root oxidises and discolours quickly so, if not frying immediately, place it in a bowl of cold water with a dash of vinegar or lemon juice until ready to use.

Heat the oil in a saucepan or deep-fryer to 170°C (340°C).

Working in batches so as not to overcrowd the pan, place the lotus root slices in the hot oil and cook for 1–2 minutes (depending on the width of your slices) until lightly golden.

Remove from the oil, drain on paper towel, then sprinkle over the sesame seed mixture. Serve hot.

Gochugaru is available from Asian supermarkets. You can substitute regular chilli powder, but use only ¼ teaspoon.

31

Masala peanuts

SERVES

4–6

2 teaspoons garlic paste

2 teaspoons ginger paste

½ teaspoon chilli powder

1 teaspoon ground turmeric

2 teaspoons garam masala

½ teaspoon salt

1 tablespoon rice flour

2 tablespoons besan
   (chickpea flour)

160 g (5½ oz/1 cup) raw peanuts,
   skins removed

vegetable or peanut oil, for
   deep-frying

In a bowl, mix together the pastes, spices, salt and flours. Add 3 teaspoons water and mix well, then add the peanuts and ½ teaspoon of oil. Using your hands, coat the peanuts with the paste. The mixture should be quite dry, and the peanuts will stick together in clumps.

Heat enough oil for deep-frying in a wok, saucepan or deep-fryer, until it reaches 160°C (320°F).

Coat the tips of your fingers in a little extra oil, so the mixture doesn't stick to them, then carefully drop the nuts into the oil, a couple at a time so that they don't all stick together. Fry, stirring occasionally, for 7–8 minutes, until the coating is golden brown.

Using a slotted spoon, remove the peanuts from the oil and drain on paper towel. Leave to cool, then serve. Store in an airtight container for up to 10 days.

It's possible that the best beer snacks in the world can be found in North India, where they're so devoted to the concept, they've given them a name. Chakhna – derived from *chakh*, meaning 'taste' – refers specifically to salted snacks served with alcoholic beverages, either at home or in a bar or restaurant. Masala peanuts are best enjoyed with a bottle of Kingfisher.

Parmesan & rosemary almonds

SERVES

6

1 egg white
25 g (1 oz/¼ cup) finely grated
  parmesan
2 teaspoons finely chopped
  rosemary
1 teaspoon garlic powder
180 g (6½ oz) blanched almonds
salt

Preheat the oven to 180°C (350°F). Line a baking tray with baking paper.

Whisk the egg white briefly until frothy.

In a bowl, combine the parmesan, rosemary, garlic powder, almonds and a good pinch of salt. Add the egg white and mix well, ensuring all the nuts get coated with some of the mixture.

Spoon the nuts onto the tray, separating them as you go. Cook in the oven for about 8 minutes, stirring once, until they are a light golden brown.

Serve warm or cold. Store in an airtight container for up to 10 days.

Sichuan almonds

Dry-fry 2 teaspoons of Sichuan peppercorns in a frying pan over low heat until fragrant, then grind into a powder. Toss 180 g (6½ oz) blanched almonds in a bowl with the ground peppercorns, ½ teaspoon sea salt flakes and 1 teaspoon olive oil. Toast in the oven as directed above.

Left: Masala peanuts (page 32); right:
Wasabi macadamia nuts with ginger (page 37)

Cashews with lemongrass, chilli & spring onion

Preheat the oven to 180°C (350°F). Line a baking tray with baking paper and lightly oil the paper.

Put all the ingredients, except for the spring onion and cashew nuts, in a small saucepan with 185 ml (6 fl oz/$\frac{3}{4}$ cup) water and bring to the boil. Leave to simmer for a few minutes until reduced to a light syrup, then remove from the heat.

Add the spring onion and cashews to the syrup and stir well to coat. Pour onto the baking tray, then roast in the oven for 5–7 minutes, stirring once, until golden.

Serve warm or cold. Store in an airtight container for up to 1 week.

SERVES

4

1 lemongrass stem, white part only, finely chopped
zest of 1 lime
1 tablespoon lime juice
¼ teaspoon salt
¼ teaspoon chilli powder
2 tablespoons grated palm sugar (jaggery)
3 spring onions (scallions), thinly sliced
150 g (5½ oz/1 cup) raw cashew nuts

Wasabi macadamia nuts with ginger

SERVES

6

3 tablespoons pickled ginger,
   drained
40 g (1½ oz) butter
2 teaspoons soy sauce
1 tablespoon wasabi paste
180 g (6½ oz) macadamia nuts
1 teaspoon wasabi powder
   (optional)

Preheat the oven to 150°C (300°F).

Place the pickled ginger between two layers of paper towel and press down to absorb some of the moisture. Place the ginger flat on a baking tray, then cook in the oven for 10 minutes, until the ginger has dried out and is crispy. Remove from the baking tray and set aside.

Increase the oven temperature to 180°C (350°F). Line a baking tray with baking paper.

Melt the butter in a small saucepan over medium heat. Remove from the heat, add the soy sauce and wasabi paste and whisk well until combined. Toss the macadamia nuts in the mixture, then pour them onto the prepared tray.

Roast in the oven for 3 minutes, then shake the tray and roast for a further 3–4 minutes, until the nuts are golden.

Remove from the oven and sift over the wasabi powder, if using. Leave to cool, then toss with the dried ginger. Store in an airtight container for 2–3 days.

These sweet–salty bacon strips
are the ultimate accompaniment to
a hearty round of good Canadian
cream stout.

Maple bacon strips

SERVES

4

12 rashers (slices) streaky bacon
125 ml (4 fl oz/½ cup) pure maple
   syrup
½ teaspoon salt
½ teaspoon freshly ground
   black pepper
2 teaspoons brown sugar

Preheat the oven to 160°C (320°F). Lightly oil a sheet of baking paper and set aside.

Lay the bacon in a single layer on a wire rack set over a baking tray.

Combine the maple syrup, salt, pepper and sugar in a small saucepan over low heat, and stir until the sugar dissolves.

Using a pastry brush, coat the bacon in the maple mixture, then place in the oven. Cook for 5 minutes, then remove, turn the bacon, baste again with the maple mixture and return to the oven for a further 5 minutes. Continue turning and basting until the bacon is crisp and a dark golden brown – it should take about 25 minutes in total. Remove from the oven.

Transfer the bacon to the oiled baking paper and leave to cool before serving.

Variation

Add a squirt of sriracha to the maple mixture, to taste.

Chilli bourbon jerky

SERVES

6

1 kg (2 lb 3 oz) lean beef

Marinade
160 ml (5½ fl oz) soy sauce
80 ml (2½ fl oz/⅓ cup)
   Worcestershire sauce
80 ml (2½ fl oz/⅓ cup) bourbon
3 teaspoons cayenne powder
1 tablespoon liquid smoke

Trim the meat of any visible fat, then pop it in a freezer bag and place in the freezer for 30–60 minutes, to firm up and make it easier to slice.

Prepare the marinade by mixing all the ingredients in a bowl. Set aside.

Remove the meat from the freezer and slice it, cutting against the grain, into very thin pieces – about 2 mm ($\frac{1}{8}$ in) thick, if possible.

Combine the beef with the marinade, cover, then leave to marinate in the fridge for about 2 hours.

Preheat the oven to 70°C (160°F).

Layer one to two pieces of paper towel on a work surface, then place the beef slices flat on the towel in a single layer. Add another couple of layers of paper on top, then press down on the towel, forcing as much marinade/moisture from the meat as possible.

Set wire racks over two or three baking trays and place the beef slices in a single layer on the racks. Transfer to the oven, using the handle of a wooden spoon to keep the oven door slightly ajar. Cook for about 3 hours, checking towards the end of the cooking time to see if the jerky is done – it should bend but not crack or crumble. Allow to cool. Store in an airtight container for up to 7 days.

This jerky is the ultimate snack to gnaw on while you knock back some PBRs and watch the Super Bowl.

Pickled eggs & potato chips

SERVES

8

8 eggs
½ teaspoon black peppercorns
1–2 dried bay leaves
310 ml (10½ fl oz/1¼ cups) white vinegar
1 tablespoon sugar
1 teaspoon salt
Potato chips (page 144), just cooked, or 2 packets of your favourite chips

Start the pickling process 3 days ahead.

Clean and sterilise a 1 litre (34 fl oz) mason or other heatproof jar.

Bring a saucepan of water to a rolling boil. Gently lower the eggs into the water and set a timer for 9 minutes. When the time is up, remove the eggs from the pan and transfer to a bowl of cold water to cool. Peel and place the eggs in the jar, along with the black peppercorns and bay leaves.

Combine the remaining ingredients, except the potato chips, in a small saucepan with 250 ml (8½ fl oz/1 cup) water and bring to the boil. Lower the heat and simmer for 2–3 minutes, stirring to dissolve the sugar and salt. Remove from the heat, leave to cool for 3–4 minutes, then pour the liquid over the eggs (you may not need all the liquid). Leave to cool, cover, then transfer the jar to the fridge. Leave to pickle for at least 2–3 days.

To serve, divide the potato chips among eight clean paper bags, pop an egg into each bag, scrunch to break it up, and enjoy!

Variation

For curried pickled eggs, add ½ teaspoon coriander seeds, ½ teaspoon ground turmeric and 1 teaspoon curry powder to the pickling liquid.

A big jar of pickled eggs is a familiar sight behind the bars of pubs throughout the UK and Ireland. When you're smashing pints and just need a little salty something, there's nothing finer.

Potato chips three ways

SERVES

4–6

Potato chips (page 144), just
   cooked

Chicken skin and thyme

70 g (2½ oz) chicken skin
sea salt flakes
freshly ground black pepper
1 teaspoon picked thyme leaves

BBQ

1 tablespoon smoked paprika
2 teaspoons garlic salt
1 teaspoon onion powder
½ teaspoon freshly ground
   black pepper
1 teaspoon caster (superfine)
   sugar
½ teaspoon cayenne pepper

Porcini and black pepper

10 g (¼ oz) dried porcini
   mushrooms
½ teaspoon freshly ground
   black pepper
½ teaspoon sea salt flakes

Prepare your chosen flavouring (see below), then set
aside while you cook the potato chips. Leave the chips to
cool for a few minutes, then toss them with the flavouring
and enjoy!

Chicken skin and thyme

Preheat the oven to 200°C (400°F). Line a baking tray with
baking paper.

Lay the skin flat on the prepared tray. Season with salt
and pepper and sprinkle over the thyme. Place another
piece of baking paper over the skin, then place another
baking tray flat on top. Roast in the oven for 10 minutes
or until crispy.

Remove the skin from the oven and leave to cool then,
along with another large pinch of sea salt flakes, grind
it roughly in a mortar and pestle.

Makes enough to season one large bowl of chips.

BBQ

Mix all the ingredients in a bowl. Makes enough seasoning
for three or four bowls of chips, so store the extra in an
airtight container for 3–4 months.

Porcini and black pepper

Put all the ingredients in a small food processor and
blend to a powder. Makes enough seasoning for two or
three bowls of chips, so store the extra in an airtight
container for 3–4 months.

Padrón peppers with lemon salt

SERVES

4

3 teaspoons sea salt flakes
zest of ½ lemon
400 g (14 oz) padrón peppers
2 tablespoons mild-flavoured
    olive oil
extra-virgin olive oil, for drizzling
lemon wedges, to serve

Combine the sea salt flakes and lemon zest in a bowl and set aside.

Rinse and dry the peppers.

Heat the olive oil to a heavy-based frying pan over high heat until shimmering, then add the peppers. Reduce the heat to medium–high heat and fry the peppers for 3–4 minutes, tossing gently so they cook on both sides. The skin will blister – when it starts to blacken in parts, they are done.

Remove from the heat, drizzle with the extra-virgin olive oil and season generously with the lemon salt. Serve with the lemon wedges.

School prawns with lime & coriander mayo

SERVES

4

vegetable oil, for deep-frying
500 g (1 lb 2 oz) school prawns
    (small shrimp)
3–4 tablespoons rice flour,
    for dusting
sea salt flakes
lime wedges, to serve

Lime & coriander mayo

zest of 1 lime
1 tablespoon lime juice
1 tablespoon chopped coriander
    (cilantro)
200 g (7 oz) whole egg
    mayonnaise
salt
freshly ground black pepper

Mix the mayo ingredients in a bowl and refrigerate until ready to serve.

Heat the oil in a saucepan or deep-fryer to 180°C (350°F).

Toss about one-third of the prawns in the rice flour, shake off the excess, then transfer to the hot oil. Cook for 2–3 minutes, until pink and crispy, then remove from the oil and drain on paper towel. Repeat with the remaining prawns and flour, then season generously with sea salt.

Serve the prawns with the mayonnaise and lime wedges.

02

21 tasty

BITES

Currywurst is undoubtedly one of Germany's most beloved beer snacks. Famously created by Herta Heuwer in Berlin in 1949, who was introduced to curry powder by British soldiers, the iconic status of currywurst only continues to grow. Serve with ice-cold German beer.

Currywurst

SERVES

4

1 tablespoon vegetable oil

1 small white onion, finely
    chopped

1 garlic clove, crushed

1 tablespoon mild curry powder,
    plus extra to serve

600 ml (20½ fl oz) passata (puréed
    tomatoes)

80 ml (2½ fl oz/⅓ cup) white wine
    vinegar

80 g (2¾ oz/⅓ cup) granulated
    sugar

2 teaspoons Worcestershire sauce

2 teaspoons salt

2 teaspoons sweet paprika

1 teaspoon mustard powder

4 Bratwurst sausages

Heat the oil in a saucepan over medium–low heat and add the onion. Cook for 3–4 minutes until soft and translucent. Add the garlic and cook for a further 2 minutes, making sure the garlic doesn't burn. Add the curry powder and cook, stirring, for 1 minute before adding the passata. Heat until simmering, then add the vinegar, sugar, Worcestershire sauce, salt, paprika and mustard powder.

Simmer, uncovered, for 15 minutes or until thickened. Remove from the heat and process with a hand-held blender until smooth.

Preheat a chargrill pan over high heat. Cook the sausages for about 20 minutes, turning occasionally, until cooked through.

To serve, cut the sausages into thick slices. Transfer to serving plates and spoon the sauce over the top. Sprinkle with extra curry powder and serve.

Crumbed garlic mussels

SERVES

4

3 garlic cloves, crushed
240 g (8½ oz) butter, at room
    temperature
140 g (5 oz) day-old bread
zest of 1 lemon
small bunch flat-leaf (Italian)
    parsley, leaves picked
freshly ground black pepper
1 kg (2 lb 3 oz) mussels, cleaned
    and debearded
lemon wedges, to serve

Combine the garlic and butter in a bowl until well combined. Set aside.

Rip the bread into chunks, then place in the bowl of a food processor, along with the lemon zest and parsley. Season with some pepper and process into coarse breadcrumbs. Set aside in a shallow bowl.

Rinse the mussels under fresh running water. Check each mussel to ensure it is closed – for any that are open, tap them on the sink or counter and they should close. Throw away any that do not close tightly. Also discard any cracked mussels.

Place the mussels in a large saucepan over high heat and add about 2 tablespoons water. Pop the lid on and cook for 5 minutes. Lift the lid and check to see if the mussels are open. If not, cover again and cook for another 1–2 minutes. Strain, and discard any mussels that have still not opened.

When the mussels have cooled slightly, take each one and separate the shells, discarding the empty shell halves.

Take one mussel and smear a generous knob of the garlic butter over it in the shell, then press it, mussel side down, into the breadcrumbs. Place on a baking tray and repeat with the remaining mussels.

Grill (broil) the mussels under a hot grill (broiler), until the breadcrumbs are golden brown and the butter is foaming. Serve with the lemon wedges.

Croquetas with Serrano ham & manchego

MAKES

20

80 g (2¾ oz) butter
200 g (7 oz/1⅓ cups) plain
    (all-purpose) flour
540 ml (18 fl oz) full-cream
    (whole) milk
100 g (3½ oz) finely grated
    manchego
100 g (3½ oz) Serrano ham,
    chopped into small pieces
2 teaspoons chopped chives
3 eggs, lightly beaten
3 teaspoons smoked paprika
120 g (4½ oz/2 cups) panko
    breadcrumbs
vegetable oil, for deep-frying

Put the butter in a small saucepan over medium heat. When foaming, add 100 g (3½ oz/⅔ cup) of the flour and cook, stirring, for 1–2 minutes. Add 500 ml (17 fl oz/2 cups) of the milk, then stir using a whisk until you have a smooth sauce with no lumps. When the mixture starts to bubble, add the manchego, ham and chives. Stir until fully melted and the sauce is quite thick and almost coming away from the side of the pan.

Pour the mixture onto a plate and place a layer of plastic wrap over the top to prevent a skin forming. Chill for 3–4 hours.

Place the beaten egg in a shallow bowl and mix in the remaining milk. In another shallow dish, place the remaining flour mixed with the paprika and stir to combine. Lastly, put the panko breadcrumbs in a third shallow dish.

Form the croquetas mixture into twenty logs, each about 40 g (1½ oz).

Dip each log into the flour to coat, then into the egg, and finally into the breadcrumbs. Re-dip in the egg and breadcrumbs, gently pressing the breadcrumbs into the logs to help them stick. Place the croquetas on a tray and return them to the fridge until the oil is ready.

Line a plate with paper towel. Heat the oil in a saucepan or deep-fryer to 170°C (340°C). Fry the croquetas in batches, four or five at a time, for 1–2 minutes, or until golden brown.

Drain on paper towel and serve hot.

Patatas bravas

SERVES

4

800 g (1 lb 12 oz) potatoes,
    scrubbed and chopped into
    chunks
3 tablespoons olive oil
2 tomatoes, halved
1 red capsicum (bell pepper),
    cut into quarters
2 teaspoons smoked paprika
¼ teaspoon chilli powder

Aïoli

2 egg yolks
2 garlic cloves, finely minced
1 teaspoon dijon mustard
250 ml (8½ fl oz/1 cup) mild-
    flavoured olive oil
1 teaspoon lemon juice or white
    wine vinegar
salt

To make the aïoli, put the yolks, garlic and mustard in the bowl of a small food processor. Process briefly. With the motor running, begin to add the oil, a couple of drops at a time, ensuring each drop is incorporated before adding the next. When all the oil is incorporated, stir in the lemon juice and season with a pinch of salt.

Preheat the oven to 180°C (350°F).

Put the potato in a saucepan of salted cold water, bring to the boil and leave to boil for 5 minutes.

Drain the potato, then transfer to a roasting tin. Leave for 4–5 minutes to dry, then add 2 tablespoons of the olive oil and toss to coat. Roast in the oven for 35–40 minutes, tossing once or twice so the potato browns easily. Season with salt.

Meanwhile, place the tomato and capsicum in a separate roasting tin. Sprinkle over the paprika and chilli powder and toss with the last tablespoon of olive oil. Place in the oven next to the potato and roast for 20 minutes. Remove the tomato and capsicum from the oven, leave to cool slightly, then blend in a food processor until you have a chunky sauce.

To serve, spread the sauce on the base of a serving plate and top with the roast potatoes. Serve the aïoli on the side for dipping.

A plate of patatas bravas is not only delicious, but necessary to line the stomach sitting in a plaza in Barcelona drinking glass after glass of cerveza.

SALUD SALUD SALUD SALUD !!!

Your guide to tapas

Whether you're gathering with friends in a plaza or hopping from bar to bar, in Spain, wherever there's a beer, there's a bite.

Free food?

Known as tapas – or *pintxos*, literally meaning 'stick', in the Basque region – these snacks were traditionally served for free with every drink. Some legends say that King Alfonso of Spain decreed that all taverns must serve a small amount of food with every alcoholic drink in order to prevent drunkenness and misconduct. Others say the king once stopped on his travels in the windy city of Seville and, in order to stop sand from blowing in his drink, he topped his glass with a plate of cured ham (tapas means 'cover', after all). There are countless stories attributing the tradition to all manner of things, but regardless, it's a practice that's hard to argue with.

While you'll still find some establishments serving simple nibbles on the house, especially in the southern regions of Spain, as modern bars have become famous for their tapas it's more common to pay. In those cases, you'll often place your drink order and bite order at the same time. Most common in the country's pintxo mecca San Sebastián, snacks are served skewered on a toothpick, which are collected and presented for payment at the end.

Look for

While tapas and pinxtos varies hugely depending on what part of the country you're in, here are a few special ones to look out for:

· Jamón ibérico de bellota – the world's finest ham, made from free-range, acorn-fed black Iberian pigs.

· Gilda – possibly the original pinxto, a Gilda is a salty skewer of anchovy, green pepper and olive. Perfection.

· Chorizo a la sidra – paprika-laced chorizo sausage cooked in dry Spanish cider.

· Pulpo a la gallega – Galician-style braised octopus.

· Gambas al ajillo – garlic prawns cooked in a clay pot, with lots of parsley and local olive oil.

· Croquetas – the ultimate beer snack of deep-fried crumbed béchamel flavoured with Serrano jamon, prawns (shrimp) or cheese.

And of course, all over Spain you'll find tapas like olives, albondigas (meatballs), patatas bravas, tortilla (Spanish omelette), garlicky clams, salt cod, salty cheeses and good old potato chips.

Albondigas

1½ tablespoons olive oil

2 large garlic cloves, thinly sliced

1 teaspoon smoked paprika

400 g (14 oz) tinned crushed
   tomatoes

6–7 basil leaves, thinly sliced

½ teaspoon sugar

salt

freshly ground black pepper

Meatballs

300 g (10½ oz) minced
   (ground) beef

300 g (10½ oz) minced
   (ground) pork

2 garlic cloves, crushed

1 teaspoon dried oregano

1 small white onion, finely diced

½ teaspoon chilli powder

75 g (2¾ oz/¾ cup) finely
   grated parmesan

1 egg, beaten

Heat ½ tablespoon of the olive oil in a saucepan over medium heat and add the garlic. Fry for a few seconds until just starting to brown, then add the paprika, tomatoes, basil, sugar and 250 ml (8½ fl oz/1 cup) water. Season to taste and stir well to combine. Bring to the boil, then reduce the heat to low and simmer for about 30 minutes, stirring occasionally, until reduced and thickened. If the mixture looks like it is beginning to get too thick, add another few tablespoons of water.

To make the meatballs, mix the ingredients in a large bowl, until well combined. Shape heaped tablespoons of the mixture into small balls – the mixture should yield about 24 meatballs.

Heat the remaining oil in a frying pan over medium heat and fry the meatballs, turning often, for 10–12 minutes, until cooked through.

Add the meatballs to the sauce and toss to coat. Serve hot.

Boquerones

SERVES

4–6

20–24 fresh anchovies
250 ml (8½ fl oz/1 cup) white
    wine vinegar
100 ml (3½ fl oz) olive oil
2 garlic cloves, finely chopped
6 pitted green olives, finely diced
½ small red capsicum
    (bell pepper), finely diced
1 tablespoon chopped flat-leaf
    parsley
salt
crusty bread, to serve

Clean the anchovies by removing the heads, splitting them down the middle and then removing the backbones and insides, keeping the fillet intact if possible. Rinse well, place in a container and put them in the freezer for 3–4 hours, or overnight, to kill off any parasites.

Remove the anchovies from the freezer and lay the fillets flat in a shallow glass dish, layering as needed depending on the size of your dish. Mix the vinegar and 60 ml (2 fl oz/¼ cup) water in a bowl, then pour over the anchovies, ensuring they are completely submerged. Cover the dish and refrigerate for 2–3 hours.

Remove the anchovies, drain the liquid and lay the fillets flat on a serving dish. Drizzle over the olive oil.

In a bowl, gently toss the garlic, olives, capsicum and parsley with a pinch of salt, then scatter the mixture over the anchovy fillets. Serve with crusty bread.

Store, covered, in the fridge, for up to 2 weeks. The fish should be completely submerged in the oil – if they are not, just top up with a bit more olive oil.

There's little that compares to the intense salty hit of punchy marinated anchovies. This classic tapa is best enjoyed with some Victoria beer at a beachside bar in Malaga.

Pork & pistachio terrine

SERVES

6–8

700 g (1 lb 9 oz) coarsely minced
  (ground) pork
300 g (10½ oz) coarsely minced
  (ground) pork fat
75 g (2¾ oz/½ cup) pistachios,
  roughly chopped
3 tablespoons cognac
½ teaspoon white pepper
¼ teaspoon ground nutmeg
¼ teaspoon ground cloves
¼ teaspoon ground cinnamon
3 teaspoons sea salt flakes
25 g (1 oz/¾ cup) chopped flat-leaf
  parsley
3 tablespoons chopped chervil
baguette, to serve (optional)

In a mixing bowl, combine the pork, pork fat, pistachios, cognac, spices and salt. Mix together well, then cover and refrigerate overnight to marinate.

The next day, preheat the oven to 180°C (350°F).

Add the parsley and chervil to the pork mixture and mix well. Transfer the mixture to a 30 cm (12 in) terrine mould (1 litre/34 fl oz/4 cup capacity), pressing down firmly. Smooth the top, cover with foil, then place the terrine in a large, deep roasting tin.

Pour enough boiling water into the roasting tin, to come halfway up the sides of the terrine mould. Transfer to the oven and bake for 1 hour.

Remove the terrine from the oven, remove the foil cover and allow to cool for 1 hour. Cover with baking paper, then place a weight on top, such as a large, square bottle of olive oil, to compress the terrine. Refrigerate overnight.

Cut the terrine into slices and serve as part of a cold platter, or in a baguette.

Chicken liver pâté

SERVES

6–8

500 g (1 lb 2 oz) chicken livers, trimmed
150 g (5½ oz) butter, chopped and softened
8 sage leaves
2 French shallots, finely chopped
80 ml (2½ fl oz/⅓ cup) brandy
salt
white pepper
thinly sliced baguette, or crackers, to serve
sliced pear, to serve

To cover the pâté

80 g (2¾ oz) unsalted butter, chopped
4 sage leaves

Place the chicken livers in a colander, rinse gently under cold water and drain. Pat dry with paper towel.

Heat about 1 tablespoon of the softened butter and four of the sage leaves in a heavy-based frying pan over medium–high heat until the butter melts and foams. Working in two batches, add the livers to the pan and cook for 3–5 minutes, until lightly browned on the outside and slightly pink on the inside. Transfer the livers to a plate.

Add the shallot and remaining sage leaves to the frying pan and cook over medium–low heat, stirring occasionally, for 5 minutes, or until the shallot is soft, adding a little more of the butter to the pan if needed.

Return the livers to the pan and add the brandy. Carefully ignite the brandy if you like. Simmer for 1 minute, or until the liquid has almost evaporated. Remove and discard the sage leaves. Leave the liver mixture to cool slightly.

Place the liver mixture in a food processor and blend until smooth, scraping down the side of the bowl if necessary. Working in batches, transfer the mixture to a coarse mesh sieve set over a bowl, and use a metal spoon to rub and push the mixture through the sieve.

Return the sieved liver mixture to the food processor with the remaining softened butter. Process, scraping down the side of the bowl as needed, until the mixture is smooth and well combined. Taste and season with salt and white pepper.

Spoon the pâté into a 400 ml (14 fl oz) dish (or several smaller dishes) and smooth the surface. Set aside.

To make the covering for the pâté, place the unsalted butter and sage leaves in a small saucepan over medium heat and cook until the butter just melts. Pour the clarified butter evenly over the surface of the pâté, leaving the white milk solids behind in the pan. Arrange the sage leaves on top. Once the butter sets, cover the pâté with plastic wrap and refrigerate overnight to set and develop the flavours.

Serve with fresh or toasted thinly sliced baguette or crackers, and slices of pear. It will keep in the fridge for up to 5 days.

Serve these fries with some kind of delicious dipping sauce (think Aïoli – page 56 – or a smoky tomato sauce) for the perfect beer snack. They also make a great side dish for any meat, especially barbecue cooked low 'n' slow.

Cheesy bacon & rosemary polenta fries

SERVES

4

250 g (9 oz) rindless loin (back) bacon, finely chopped

1 teaspoon finely chopped rosemary

1 litre (34 fl oz/4 cups) vegetable stock

210 g (7½ oz) instant (fine) polenta

100 g (3½ oz/1 cup) finely grated parmesan

salt

freshly ground black pepper

vegetable oil, for deep-frying

finely chopped flat-leaf (Italian) parsley, to serve

salt flakes, to serve

Line a 33 cm × 23 cm (13 in × 9 in) baking tray with baking paper.

Cook the bacon in a large non-stick frying pan over medium heat for 6–8 minutes until browned and slightly crisp. Add the rosemary to the pan and stir for 1 minute. Transfer the bacon and rosemary to a plate.

Bring the stock to the boil in a large heavy-based saucepan over medium heat. Slowly whisk in the polenta. Stir for 2 minutes, or until thickened. Remove from the heat and stir in the bacon mixture and the cheese. Season with salt and pepper. Spoon the polenta over the prepared tray and set aside for 2–3 hours until set.

Turn out the polenta onto a work surface and trim the edges. Slice into 2 cm ($\frac{3}{4}$ in) strips (you should get about sixteen), then cut each in half.

Heat the oil in a saucepan or deep-fryer to 190°C (375°F). Deep-fry the polenta fries in small batches for 2–3 minutes, until golden. Drain on paper towel.

Sprinkle with parsley and salt flakes and serve.

Variation

To make these a bit more posh, sprinkle liberally with smoked or truffled salt.

Samosas

MAKES

12

2 medium potatoes, about 300 g
 (10½ oz) in total
80 g (2¾ oz/½ cup) frozen peas
½ teaspoon coriander seeds
½ teaspoon cumin seeds
vegetable oil
¼ teaspoon mustard seeds
¼ onion, diced
1 green chilli, finely chopped
1 teaspoon ginger paste
1 garlic clove, minced
¼ teaspoon ground turmeric
1 teaspoon garam masala
2 teaspoons mango chutney
2 tablespoons chopped coriander
 (cilantro)

Dough

360 g (12½ oz) plain (all-purpose)
 flour
½ teaspoon salt
1 teaspoon nigella or cumin seeds
 (optional)
60 ml (2 fl oz/¼ cup) vegetable oil
 or melted ghee

Raita

250 g (9 oz/1 cup) plain yoghurt
1 small Lebanese (short)
 cucumber, grated
small handful of mint leaves,
 chopped
salt
freshly ground black pepper

To make the dough, mix together the flour, salt, seeds (if using) and oil until the mixture resembles breadcrumbs. Turn the dough out onto a clean work surface, make a small well in the centre and pour in 100 ml (3½ fl oz) of warm water. Bring it all together to form a dough, adding another tablespoon of water if needed. Knead well for 5–7 minutes until you have a smooth dough.

Roll the dough into a log and then divide it into six even pieces. Roll each portion into a ball, then place on a tray, cover with plastic wrap and leave to rest in the fridge for about 1 hour.

To make the raita, mix the ingredients together in a small bowl. Set aside.

Put the potatoes in a saucepan, cover with cold water and bring to the boil. Boil for 10–15 minutes, until cooked through. Remove from the water, slip off the skins and cut the potatoes into 1 cm (½ in) dice. Set aside.

Put the peas in a heatproof bowl and cover with boiling water. Leave for 3–4 minutes, then drain and set aside with the potato.

Dry-fry the coriander and cumin seeds in a frying pan over medium heat, then grind in a food processor or mortar and pestle.

Heat 1 tablespoon of oil in a frying pan over medium–high heat, add the mustard seeds and cook for 30 seconds until they start to pop. Add the onion, chilli, ginger, garlic, ground cumin and coriander seeds, turmeric and garam masala to the pan and fry for 3–4 minutes, stirring often. Add the peas, potato and 250 ml (8½ fl oz/1 cup) water. Reduce the heat to low and leave to simmer for 4–5 minutes, until the liquid has reduced. Remove from the heat, stir in the mango chutney and chopped coriander, then leave to cool while you roll the dough.

Working with one dough ball at a time, roll the dough into a long oval shape about 2 mm ($\frac{1}{8}$ in) thick. Cut the oval in half crossways. Take one half, dab some water along the cut side, then curve the cut sides around to meet, joining them together to make a cone shape. Press the cut sides to seal well. Pile a heaped teaspoon of the filling mixture into the cone, then dab some water around the rim of the pastry and fold over the curved side, again pressing well to seal and then curling up the edges. Make another samosa with the other half of the oval and repeat the process with the remaining dough and filling.

Heat enough oil for deep-frying in a saucepan or deep-fryer to 170°C (340°C) and fry the samosas, three or four at a time, for 6–8 minutes, until golden brown. Serve hot or cold with the raita.

Samosas are probably India's most iconic street food and for good reason. It's a simple concept – filling wrapped in dough and then deep-fried – with endless potential for variation. This recipe is a fairly classic vegetarian version, but you can stuff samosas with minced (ground) lamb and peas, prawns, dal or paneer. Whatever takes your fancy.

Devils on horseback

SERVES

4

70 g (2½ oz) hard blue cheese, such as stilton or Danish blue
1 tablespoon chopped almonds, toasted
16 soft prunes or dates, pitted
8 rashers (slices) streaky bacon
olive oil, for brushing

Preheat the oven to 180°C (350°F).

Crumble the cheese into a bowl and mix with the chopped almonds.

Gently push your finger into the hole left by the pit in the prune, and wiggle it around to create a small cavity for the stuffing. Push as much of the blue cheese mixture as will fit in the cavity – you don't want to split the side of the prune but if this does happen, it's easily covered up with bacon.

Cut each rasher of bacon in half.

Lay a slice of bacon in front of you, place a stuffed prune at one end, then roll it up, securing with a toothpick. Brush a little oil over each roll, then place on a baking tray. Repeat with the remaining ingredients and roast for 10–12 minutes until the bacon is crisp and cooked through. Serve warm.

Don't discount a classic. Devils on horseback are pure retro gold – salty, smoky and sweet – and, as such, pair perfectly with a light beer sipped at a swingers' party – or a regular beer at a regular party. You do you.

Seaweed tempura

SERVES

4

ice cubes
140 ml (4½ fl oz) soda water
   (club soda), chilled
6 nori sheets
vegetable oil, for deep-frying
30 g (1 oz/¼ cup) cornflour
   (cornstarch)
35 g (1¼ oz/¼ cup) plain
   (all-purpose) flour
¼ teaspoon bicarbonate of soda
   (baking soda)
1 egg yolk
2 tablespoons sesame seeds

Add the ice cubes to the soda water and leave to chill for 5 minutes.

Dab the edges of the nori with water and fold each sheet in half. Cut each half into five rectangular strips.

Heat the oil in a saucepan or deep-fryer to 190°C (375°F).

In order to keep the batter as cold as possible, make an ice bath for it. Put some cold water in a large bowl, add some ice cubes, then set a smaller bowl – big enough to make the batter in – inside the larger bowl.

Sift the flours and bicarbonate of soda together into the smaller bowl.

Measure out 140 ml (4½ fl oz) of the soda water and mix with the egg yolk in a small bowl. Add the mixture to the flour and stir quickly until combined – a few lumps in the batter are fine.

Working quickly, dip a piece of nori into the batter, sprinkle with a few sesame seeds, then carefully lower into the oil. Fry for 10–15 seconds, until the batter has puffed up and is a light golden brown. Drain the nori on paper towel, then repeat with the remaining ingredients.

Serve immediately.

It's best to make the batter as the oil is heating, so that it's as cold as possible when you cook it.

KAMPAI
KAMPAI !!!
KAMPAI !!!
KAMPAI !!!

A night in a yakitori bar

Follow your nose down a small street in Tokyo
and you'll likely stumble across one of the city's
countless tiny yakitori bars.

A late night repast

A mainstay of late-finishing salarymen looking for an after-work beer and bite to eat before their commute home, yakitori translates to 'grilled chicken' — and in Japan, this means pretty much every part of the bird. Heart, skin, intestine, liver and cartilage all grace the grill, along with the more common thigh and wing cuts. Yakitori are cooked on a small charcoal grill called a hibachi, ensuring smoky perfection.

Ordering

In a yakitori bar you order by the stick. In Japanese: *ippon* – one stick; *nihon* – two sticks; *sanbon* – three sticks; *yonhon* – four sticks.

You may be asked if you want shio or tare. Shio is salty and tare is a sweet sauce similar to teriyaki sauce.

Drinking

Tokyo locals love their beer and you'll see the big brands Asahi, Kirin, and Sapporo everywhere. If you're sharing a pitcher, it's considered polite to fill everyone else's glasses and not your own. You should wait for someone else to fill your glass, usually after you've done the same for them.

Tsukune

Soak 20 bamboo skewers in water for 30 minutes.

To make the sauce, place the ingredients in a small saucepan, bring to the boil, then reduce the heat and leave to simmer for about 10 minutes, until the sauce thickens slightly. Set aside.

MAKES

10

Place the shiitake mushrooms in a small bowl and cover with boiling water. Leave for 20 minutes, then drain the mushrooms and squeeze out the excess liquid. Roughly chop.

4 dried shiitake mushrooms
boiling water
200 g (7 oz) boneless skinless
    chicken breasts, roughly
    chopped
300 g (10½ oz) boneless skinless
    chicken thighs, roughly
    chopped
3 spring onions (scallions),
    2 roughly chopped and
    1 thinly sliced
2 teaspoons red miso paste
3 garlic cloves, minced
2 teaspoons minced ginger
½ teaspoon white pepper
¼ teaspoon salt
1 teaspoon sesame oil
1 teaspoon sesame seeds, toasted

Place the mushroom, chicken and the two roughly chopped spring onions in the bowl of a food processor and process until finely chopped and there are no big chunks of chicken left.

Transfer the mixture to a bowl and add the miso, garlic, ginger, white pepper, salt and sesame oil. Using your hands, knead the mixture well until all the ingredients are combined.

Divide the mixture into 10 balls. Place one ball in the palm of your hand, then push two skewers into the meat and wrap the meat around them in a sausage shape. Repeat with the remaining balls and skewers.

Sauce

125 ml (4 fl oz/½ cup) soy sauce
30 g (1 oz) brown sugar
80 ml (2½ fl oz/⅓ cup) sake
125 ml (4 fl oz/½ cup) mirin

Cook the skewers under a hot grill (broiler) for 5 minutes, then flip and cook for another 5 minutes. Flip again and this time, using a pastry brush, baste the meat with the sauce. Pop the skewers back under the grill for 1 minute, then flip and baste the other side. Repeat until the chicken is cooked through.

Serve the skewers with the remaining sauce drizzled over the top and sprinkled with the sesame seeds and thinly sliced spring onion.

Anyone who has squeezed into a tiny yakitori bar and partied with tipsy businessmen in Tokyo in a thick, delicious haze of hibachi smoke will understand the magic of tsukune.

In Hanoi, the cornershop bia hoi is almost good, almost cold and almost free. Pull up a tiny blue stool and dive into a plate of spring rolls to temper tomorrow's inevitable hangover.

Spring rolls with nuoc cham

MAKES

14–16

3 dried shiitake mushrooms
2 pieces dried cloud ear fungus
(optional)
boiling water
75 g (2¾ oz) minced (ground) pork
125 g (4½ oz) prawn (shrimp) meat
2 spring onions (scallions), sliced
1 garlic clove
1 coriander (cilantro) stalk, finely
chopped
40 g (1½ oz/¼ cup) finely grated carrot
15 g (½ oz/¼ cup) finely shredded
cabbage
¾ teaspoon minced ginger
½ teaspoon sesame oil
1 teaspoon soy sauce
¼ teaspoon white pepper
½ teaspoon rice wine vinegar
14–16 x 12 cm (4¾ in) spring roll
wrappers
vegetable or peanut oil, for deep-frying
fresh herbs, such as mint or Vietnamese
mint, to serve

Nuoc cham

3 teaspoons grated palm sugar
1 garlic clove, finely chopped
2 tablespoons fish sauce
60 ml (2 fl oz/¼ cup) lime juice
1 bird's eye chilli, thinly sliced
1 tablespoon finely grated carrot

To make the nuoc cham, combine all the ingredients in a small saucepan with 80 ml (2½ fl oz/⅓ cup) water over low heat for 3–4 minutes. Set aside.

Put the shiitake mushrooms and cloud ear fungus (if using) in a small bowl and cover with boiling water. Leave for 20 minutes, then drain the mushrooms and squeeze out the excess liquid. Roughly chop.

Place the mushroom, fungus, pork, prawns, spring onion and garlic in the bowl of a food processor and process until finely chopped.

Transfer the mixture to a bowl and add the coriander, carrot, cabbage, ginger, sesame oil, soy sauce, white pepper and rice wine vinegar. Using your hands, knead the mixture well, until all the ingredients are combined.

Working with one wrapper at a time laid out like a diamond in front of you, spoon a heaped teaspoon of the mixture onto one corner of the wrapper (the 'south'), and mould the filling into a short sausage shape. Fold up the 'south' corner of the wrapper and roll it halfway. Fold in the two side corners 'east' and 'west', then roll it closed, using a dab of water to seal. Place the spring rolls on a tray and cover with a damp cloth while you repeat with the rest of the filling and wrappers.

Heat the oil in a saucepan or deep-fryer to 190°C (375°F), and cook the spring rolls in batches, four or five at a time, for 5 minutes, or until crisp and cooked through.

Serve hot with the nuoc cham and fresh herbs.

Salt & pepper tofu

SERVES

4–6

400 g (14 oz) medium tofu
2 teaspoons Sichuan peppercorns
1 teaspoon salt
1 tablespoon cornflour
    (cornstarch)
2 tablespoons plain (all-purpose)
    flour
vegetable oil, for frying

Dipping sauce

2 tablespoons lemon juice
2 tablespoons light soy sauce
1 tablespoon finely chopped
    coriander (cilantro)
1 long red chilli, thinly sliced

Mix all the ingredients for the dipping sauce together. Set aside to let the flavours develop.

Place the tofu on a few layers of paper towel, top with some more paper towel, then place a plate on top. Put a weight on the plate – a 400 g (14 oz) tin of something works well. Leave for 20 minutes to draw out some of the moisture from the tofu.

Cut the tofu into 2 cm ($\frac{3}{4}$ in) bite-sized cubes. Set aside.

Dry-fry the peppercorns in a frying pan over low heat until fragrant. Transfer to a mortar, add the salt and grind into a coarse powder using the pestle.

Combine the flours and the pepper mixture in a zip lock bag. Add half the tofu, seal and shake gently, so that the tofu is fully coated in the flour mixture. Remove the tofu from the bag and shake off the excess flour – this is most easily done by putting the tofu in a dry colander. Repeat with the remaining tofu.

Pour enough oil into a large frying pan to come about 3 cm ($1\frac{1}{4}$ in) up the side. Alternatively, you can use a deep-fryer. Heat the oil to 180°C (350°F). Carefully add half the tofu and fry for 4–6 minutes until lightly golden. Remove from the heat and drain on paper towel. Repeat with the remaining tofu.

Serve straight away with the dipping sauce on the side.

Korean corn cheese

SERVES

4–6

kernels from 3 corn cobs
30 g (1 oz) butter
2 tablespoons mayonnaise
salt
150 g (5½ oz) mozzarella, grated
1 spring onion (scallion), thinly
    sliced

Heat the butter in a cast-iron frying pan over medium heat and add the corn. Fry the corn for 7–10 minutes, until the corn takes on a little colour. Remove the pan from the heat and stir through the mayonnaise and a pinch of salt. Top with the grated mozzarella.

Preheat a grill (broiler) to high, then place the pan under the grill and cook until the cheese is melted and bubbling.

Serve while the cheese is still bubbling, garnished with the spring onion.

Variation

For a hit of heat, when the corn is done, add 1 tablespoon chilli paste and ½ teaspoon sugar to the corn and fry for another 2 minutes. Add 3 tablespoons water and cook until the mixture is reduced slightly. Top with the mozzarella and grill.

If you don't have a cast-iron pan, you can just transfer the corn to any oven-safe dish before topping with mozzarella and grilling (broiling).

Tteokbokki

6–8

600 g (1 lb 5 oz) rice cakes
(available from Asian
supermarkets)
3 tablespoons gochujang
chilli paste
2 tablespoons sugar
45 ml (1½ fl oz) soy sauce
2–3 spring onions (scallions),
thinly sliced

Prepare the rice cakes according to the packet instructions. If using fresh, cut them into 3 cm (1¼ in) lengths before cooking. Set aside.

Place a wok or large frying pan over medium-high heat, add the chilli paste, sugar, soy sauce and 600 ml (20½ fl oz) water. Mix well and bring to the boil. Add the rice cakes, return to the boil, then reduce the heat and leave to simmer for 8–10 minutes, until the sauce is thick and coats the rice cakes.

Remove and serve, sprinkled with the sliced spring onion.

The late-night streets of Seoul are lined with vendors selling these rice cakes, or 'tteokbokki'. Fun to say, fun to eat – you'll need a big pint of maekju to cool the heat of the fiery gochujang in this dish.

Son-in-law eggs

SERVES

6

6 eggs, at room temperature
iced water
vegetable oil, for deep-frying
small handful of coriander
(cilantro) leaves
1 long red chilli, thinly sliced
lengthways

Crispy shallots

125 ml (4 fl oz/½ cup) peanut oil
2 Asian shallots, thinly sliced

Tamarind sauce

90 g (3 oz) tamarind pulp
(concentrate)
30 ml (1 fl oz) fish sauce
2 tablespoons grated palm sugar
(jaggery)

To make the crispy shallots, place the peanut oil and shallots in a wok over medium–high heat. Fry for 5–6 minutes, until the shallots are a light golden colour, then remove using a slotted spoon and drain on paper towel. The shallots will get crispy as they cool.

Bring a saucepan of water to a rolling boil. Gently lower the eggs into the water and set a timer for 8 minutes – this will yield a semi-soft yolk; boil for an extra 2 minutes for a firmer yolk. When the time is up, remove the eggs from the pan and place them in a bowl of iced water. Leave to cool for about 5 minutes, then gently peel the eggs, taking care not to break them, and pat them dry.

To make the tamarind sauce, combine the ingredients in a saucepan over medium heat, then stir until the sugar has dissolved and the sauce has thickened.

In a saucepan or deep-fryer, heat the oil to 170°C (340°C) and deep-fry the eggs for 4–5 minutes until they are crispy and golden all over.

Serve the eggs with the tamarind sauce spooned over the top, along with the coriander, chilli and crispy shallots sprinkled.

When ordering these from a street food vendor in Thailand, a large bottle of Singha in hand, you'll want to ask for 'kai loug kheuh'. According to legend, the dish was created by a protective mother as a warning to her no-good son-in-law that if he didn't treat her daughter right, he'd find his bits similarly fried and sliced!

Cheesy jalapeño & bacon twists

MAKES

12

2 sheets (about 350 g/12½ oz)
   butter puff pastry, just thawed
1 egg, lightly beaten
90 g (3 oz/¾ cup) grated vintage
   cheddar
25 g (1 oz/¼ cup) grated parmesan
1 tablespoon roughly chopped
   pickled jalapeños
1 tablespoon dijon mustard
6 rashers (slices) rindless streaky
   bacon, halved lengthways
sesame seeds, to sprinkle

Preheat the oven to 180°C (350°F). Line two large baking trays with baking paper.

Place one sheet of puff pastry on a chopping board. Brush with the egg and sprinkle with the cheeses and jalapeños. Brush the remaining sheet of pastry with egg and place, egg side down, over the cheese-covered pastry. Press down on the pastry, firmly but gently, all over so it sticks together. Spread the top with the mustard and cut into twelve even strips.

Gently separate one of the pastry strips, press a slice of bacon onto the top and twist. Place on the prepared baking tray, then repeat with the remaining bacon and pastry. Brush each twist with a little more egg and sprinkle with sesame seeds.

Bake for 15 minutes until golden. Carefully turn the twists and bake for a further 5–8 minutes, until the bacon is cooked through. Remove from the oven and cool slightly before diving in.

You can cool these twists on a wire rack and serve them at room temperature, but they're best eaten within an hour or two of baking.

Sweet potato oven fries

SERVES

4–6

vegetable oil, for greasing
800 g (1 lb 12 oz) sweet potatoes,
   scrubbed
1½ teaspoons smoked paprika
1 teaspoon garlic powder
1 teaspoon picked thyme leaves
sea salt
freshly ground black pepper
2 tablespoons olive oil

Chipotle sour cream

200 g (7 oz) sour cream
1 chipotle chilli in adobo sauce,
   chopped, plus 1 teaspoon of
   the sauce
juice of ½ lime

For the chipotle sour cream, combine the ingredients in a bowl, then refrigerate until needed.

Preheat the oven to 200°C (400°F). Lightly grease two baking trays with oil.

Cut the sweet potatoes into even-sized batons, about 1 cm (½ in) wide, then transfer to a large bowl. Sprinkle over the paprika, garlic powder and thyme, then season with salt and pepper. Add the oil, then mix everything together until the potato is evenly coated.

Divide the potato between the two trays – they should be in a single layer and not touching. Bake for 30–35 minutes, turning once halfway during cooking, until cooked through and golden brown at the edges.

Serve hot with the chipotle sour cream.

Scotch eggs

MAKES

6

6 eggs, at room temperature
iced water
500 g (1 lb 2 oz) good-quality pork
  sausages
1 teaspoon mustard powder
¼ teaspoon salt
½ teaspoon freshly ground black
  pepper
4 tablespoons plain (all-purpose)
  flour
1 egg, beaten with 2 teaspoons
  milk
90 g (3 oz/1½ cups) panko
  breadcrumbs
vegetable oil
mustard (optional)

Bring a saucepan of water to a rolling boil. Gently lower
the eggs into the water and set a timer for 8 minutes –
this will yield a semi-soft yolk; boil for an extra
2 minutes for a firmer yolk. When the time is up, remove
the eggs from the pan and place them in a bowl of iced
water. Leave to cool for about 5 minutes, then gently
peel the eggs, taking care not to break them, as they
will still be quite soft.

Remove the sausages from their casing, add the mustard
powder, salt and pepper and mash the meat briefly. Divide
into six even portions.

Put the flour, beaten egg and milk and the breadcrumbs
in three separate shallow dishes.

Working gently, roll the eggs first in the flour, then
wrap a portion of sausage meat around them, ensuring that
no egg is peeking through.

Dip the sausage-wrapped eggs back in the flour to coat,
then in the beaten egg, and lastly in the breadcrumbs. Cup
each egg in your hands and gently press the breadcrumbs
into the sausage meat to ensure they stick.

Heat enough oil for deep-frying in a medium saucepan
or deep-fryer to 170°C (340°C). Deep-fry the eggs,
two or three at a time, for about 7 minutes, or until
golden brown.

Remove the eggs with a slotted spoon and leave to drain
for a few minutes on paper towel.

Eat hot, warm or cold. A good smear of mustard makes a
fine friend.

Variation

Instead of plain pork sausages, try using your favourite
spicy Italian-style sausages and substituting 1 teaspoon
of smoked paprika for the mustard powder.

When you're perched at the bar in an 18th-century English country pub, with a roaring fire to your left and a pint of hand-pumped ale in front of you, all you need to complete the picture is a plate of Scotch eggs.

Beer & cheese dip

SERVES

6–8

1 tablespoon olive oil

10 g (⅓ oz) butter

125 g (4½ oz) trimmed bacon rashers (slices), cut into thin strips

1 onion, thinly sliced

1 garlic clove, crushed

100 g (3½ oz) camembert

60 g (2 oz/½ cup) grated Swiss cheese

60 g (2 oz/½ cup) grated smoked or vintage cheddar

1 tablespoon plain (all-purpose) flour

3 tablespoons panko breadcrumbs

2 spring onions (scallions), thinly sliced

80 ml (2½ fl oz/⅓ cup) German beer, any variety

pinch of smoked hot paprika

Pretzels (page 138), to serve

Preheat the oven to 180°C (350°F).

Heat the oil and butter in a large heavy-based frying pan over medium–high heat. Cook the bacon, onion and garlic, stirring frequently, for 8–10 minutes, until the bacon is lightly browned and the onion and garlic are golden. Remove from the heat and set aside to cool for 5 minutes.

Depending on the ripeness of the cheese, chop or mash the camembert (including the rind). Transfer to a large bowl and add the Swiss cheese, cheddar and flour. Toss to combine, then add the breadcrumbs, spring onion, beer and half the bacon mixture. Spoon into a 500 ml (17 fl oz/2 cup) capacity ovenproof dish and scatter over the remaining bacon mixture and the paprika. Bake for 20–25 minutes, until the cheese is melted and the top golden.

Serve immediately with pretzels.

Guacamole

4–6

¼ small white onion, finely
    chopped
½ fresh jalapeño, seeded and
    finely chopped
large handful of coriander
    (cilantro), stalks and leaves
    chopped separately
sea salt
2 ripe avocados
juice of ½ lime, plus extra to taste
freshly ground black pepper
Classic tortilla chips (page 143),
    to serve

Using a mortar and pestle, pound the onion, jalapeño and chopped coriander stalks with a pinch of salt, or crush with a fork on a chopping board.

Cut the avocados in half and discard the stones. Scoop out the flesh and place it in a bowl. Add the onion mixture, lime juice and a generous pinch of salt and pepper. Roughly mash the mixture together with a whisk or fork. (Using a whisk may sound a bit strange, but it works really well. It's super quick and roughly chops up the avocado, leaving a good amount of texture.)

Fold in the chopped coriander leaves. Season to taste with a little more salt, pepper and/or lime juice.

Serve immediately with the tortilla chips, or press a double layer of plastic wrap over the surface of the guacamole and refrigerate until required. It will keep in the fridge for up to 2 days.

Roasted garlic guacamole

Preheat the oven to 180°C (350°F). Remove any loose papery skin from the outside of one whole garlic bulb, then trim off the top 5 mm ($\frac{1}{4}$ in) of the bulb, leaving the bulb intact. Place it on a square of foil, cut side up, drizzle 1 tablespoon of olive oil over the cut surface and sprinkle with a little salt. Wrap the foil around the garlic and place directly on an oven shelf. Roast for 35–40 minutes, or until soft. Remove from the oven and set aside to cool. Squeeze out the roasted garlic flesh and stir it through the onion mixture before adding to the avocado as above.

Tomatillo guacamole

Add three chopped roasted (or tinned) tomatillos to the mixture.

Chipotle guacamole

Stir in one chopped chipotle chilli in adobo sauce, along with 1–2 teaspoons of the adobo sauce.

Refried beans

SERVES

6

80 ml (2½ fl oz/⅓ cup) vegetable
   oil or lard
1 small onion, peeled and halved
50 g (1¾ oz) piece of salted
   smoked pork (optional)
600 g (1 lb 5 oz/3½ cups) cooked
   pinto or black beans
approximately 170 ml
   (5½ fl oz/⅔ cup) reserved
   cooking liquid from the beans,
   or chicken stock or water
sea salt
crumbled cheese, such as cotija,
   Oaxaca, queso fresco, feta,
   mozzarella or ricotta, to serve
Classic tortilla chips (page 143),
   to serve

Warm the oil in a cast-iron pan over medium heat. Add the onion and smoked pork, if using. Heat through to flavour the oil for 1–2 minutes, then remove from the pan and reserve for another use.

Add the beans and stir through the flavoured oil, then cook for about 5–8 minutes.

Smash the beans with a potato masher or the back of a large spoon. Add the reserved bean cooking liquid or stock as needed, to achieve the desired consistency and creaminess, cooking for a further 4–5 minutes to warm the beans through.

Season to taste with sea salt and serve immediately with a sprinkling of cheese and some tortilla chips.

Clockwise from bottom left:
Refried beans (page 99),
Pico de gallo (page 103),
Guacamole (page 98),
Roasted tomato salsa (page 102)

Roasted tomato salsa

SERVES

4–6

6 roma (plum) tomatoes, cored
¼ white onion, roughly chopped
1 small garlic clove, peeled
½ fresh jalapeño (for a milder
    salsa, remove the seeds
    and membranes)
salt and freshly ground black
    pepper
Classic tortilla chips (page 143),
    to serve

Preheat the oven to 210°C (410°F).

Put the tomatoes in a roasting tin and cook in the oven for 20 minutes, or until the skin is wrinkled and the tomatoes are starting to collapse and char. Remove from the oven and set aside to cool slightly. Peel away and discard the skins.

Blend or process the onion, garlic and jalapeño until almost puréed. Add the tomatoes and blend until just combined. Season to taste with salt and pepper.

Serve warm or cold with tortilla chips.

The salsa will keep in an airtight container in the fridge for up to 4 days.

Roasted garlic and tomato salsa

Add the garlic clove to the roasting tin with the tomatoes.

Roasted capsicum, onion and tomato salsa

Quarter a red capsicum (bell pepper) and an onion and add to the roasting tin with the tomatoes.

Pico de gallo

SERVES

4–6

3 large ripe tomatoes, finely
   chopped
½ teaspoon salt, plus extra
   to taste
½ white onion, finely chopped
1–2 fresh serrano chillies or
   jalapeños, finely chopped
   (deseeded for a milder salsa)
25 g (1 oz/½ cup) finely chopped
   coriander (cilantro) leaves
1 tablespoon lime juice
Classic tortilla chips (page 143),
   to serve

Toss the tomato and salt together in a colander or sieve set over a bowl. Allow to drain for 20–30 minutes, then discard the liquid.

Combine the drained tomato with the onion, chilli, coriander and lime juice. Toss to combine and season to taste with salt. Serve with tortilla chips.

The pico de gallo can be stored in an airtight container for up to 3 days in the fridge.

You can prepare this recipe without salting the tomato. The flavour won't be quite as intense, but it will still taste good!

Queso con chorizo

SERVES

4–6

3 fresh jalapeños
2 teaspoons oil
½ onion, diced
2 garlic cloves, crushed
1 fresh chorizo sausage, diced
6–8 cherry tomatoes, quartered
220 g (8 oz) cheddar, grated
2 tablespoons milk, plus extra
   if needed
75 g (2¾ oz) cream cheese
handful of coriander (cilantro)
   leaves, roughly chopped
Classic tortilla chips (page 143),
   to serve

Blacken two of the jalapeños over a gas flame, until blistered. Leave to cool, then chop into small pieces.

Heat the oil in a cast-iron frying pan over medium heat, then add the onion, garlic and chorizo. Fry for 2–3 minutes, then add half the tomato and continue to cook for a further minute. Add the blackened jalapeños and the cheddar, allowing the cheese to melt slightly, then stir in the milk and cream cheese. Continue to stir until the cheese has melted – you can loosen the sauce with an extra splash of milk, if needed.

Remove the pan from the heat, garnish with the chopped coriander, the remaining cherry tomato and the last jalapeño, cut into thin slices.

Serve warm with tortilla chips.

This is a Tex–Mex take on fondue. It's a big bowl of spicy, hot cheese served with tortilla chips. What more could you possibly want? (Maybe a Lone Star beer to wash it down.)

SAY CHEESE !!! SAY CHEESE !!! SAY CHEESE !!! SAY CHEESE !!! SAY CHEESE !!! SAY CHEESE !!!

Matching beer and cheese

Wine and cheese gets all the glory, but in actual fact beer makes for a much better match (there's a reason why there are so many cheese-focused recipes in this book). Here's a quick guide to some favourite pairings.

Chevre

For a light goat's cheese like chevre, you want something citrussy,
such as Belgian or German witber, or a saison. The bright orangey
tanginess is a perfect complement. Greek feta made from goat's milk
also works well in this pairing.

Comte

This French sheep's milk cheese has some distinctly nutty
characteristics, so it works beautifully with a brown or amber ale –
anything with rich, toasty, caramel flavours. Other nutty cheeses
like gouda, as well as other sheep's milk cheeses from the Alpine and
Pyrenees regions work well here, too.

Cheddar

For a nice sharp cheddar, try something with a good hit of bitterness,
such as particularly hoppy IPA. Aside from cheddar, IPA pairs
particularly well with any especially creamy cheese – such as a triple
cream brie or a delice – as the bitterness cuts through the richness.

Blue cheese

For a nice creamy, stinky blue, you can't go past an imperial stout.
A stout with chocolate or hazelnut flavours makes for the ideal match,
with the blue's salty creaminess really bringing out the sweetness in
the beer.

Brie

Soft-ripened cheeses like brie or camembert are often quite mild
in flavour, making them a great option to pair with a large range
of beers. A classic pairing is with a farmhouse saison – the funkier
the better – to bring out any earthy, mushroomy qualities
in the cheese.

Herb & roasted garlic goat's cheese

SERVES

4–6

1 whole garlic bulb
1 teaspoon olive oil
salt
200 g (7 oz) soft marinated
    goat's cheese
100 g (3½ oz) cream cheese,
    softened
3 tablespoons chopped herbs,
    such as flat-leaf (Italian) parsley,
    tarragon and chives
sea salt flakes
white pepper
baguette slices and crudités,
    to serve

Preheat the oven to 180°C (350°F).

Remove any loose papery skin from the outside of the garlic bulb, then trim off the top 5 mm (¼ in) of the bulb, leaving the bulb intact. Place the garlic bulb on a square of foil, cut side up, drizzle the olive oil over the cut surface and sprinkle with a little salt. Wrap the foil around the garlic and place it directly on an oven shelf. Roast for 35–40 minutes, or until soft. Remove from the oven and set aside to cool.

Squeeze the roasted garlic cloves out of their skins and place in a food processor. Add the cheeses and herbs and blend until smooth, scraping down the side of the bowl if necessary. Taste and season with salt and white pepper.

Transfer to a small airtight container and refrigerate until required. This cheese will keep in the fridge for up to 7 days.

Serve with the baguette slices and crudites.

Dal bhat

SERVES

4–6

200 g (7 oz/1 cup) masoor dal
   (split red lentils), well rinsed
½ teaspoon salt
40 g (1½ oz) ghee
1 onion, chopped
½ teaspoon ground coriander
½ teaspoon ground cumin
½ teaspoon chilli powder
½ teaspoon ground turmeric
¼ teaspoon ground cardamom
¼ teaspoon ground cinnamon
pinch of ground cloves
Roti canai (page 140) or Simple
   naan (page 141), to serve

Combine the masoor dal and salt with 375 ml (12½ fl oz/1½ cups) of water in a saucepan over medium heat and bring to the boil. Reduce the heat to a low simmer, then cover, leaving the lid open a crack, and cook, stirring occasionally, for 20–25 minutes, until the lentils are soft and broken down. Add a little more boiling water if the mixture starts to stick to the bottom of the pan or if it's becoming too thick – the finished dal should be quite soupy.

Meanwhile, heat the ghee in a small frying pan over medium heat. Add the onion and cook, stirring occasionally, for 8–10 minutes, until golden. Add the spices and cook for 2–3 minutes, until fragrant. Stir the spice mixture into the dal.

Serve with roti or naan.

Satay dip

SERVES

4

5 dried red chillies

boiling water

1 lemongrass stalk, white part only

3 garlic cloves

2–3 cm (¾–1¼ in) knob of ginger

2–3 cm (¾–1¼ in) knob of galangal

2 Asian shallots

80 ml (2½ fl oz/⅓ cup) vegetable oil

70 g (2½ oz) smooth peanut butter

2 tablespoons grated palm sugar (jaggery)

30 ml (1 fl oz) lime juice, plus extra is needed

Roti canai (page 140) or Simple naan (page 141), to serve

Place the chillies in a small bowl, cover with boiling water and leave to soak for about 10 minutes. Drain.

Roughly chop the chillies, lemongrass, garlic, ginger, galangal and shallots, then blend to a fine paste in a small food processor or a blender. If you like, you can add a tablespoon of the oil to the paste to help give it a smoother consistency.

Heat the remaining oil in a saucepan over medium heat. Add the paste and fry for 10–12 minutes, stirring often, until the oil begins to separate from the paste and the paste is darker in colour.

Add 250 ml (8½ fl oz/1 cup) of water, the peanut butter, palm sugar and lime juice and mix well. Bring to the boil, then reduce the heat to low and leave to simmer for about 10 minutes, stirring occasionally to make sure it doesn't catch at the bottom. Taste and adjust the seasoning if needed, adding more lime juice or sugar to suit your preference.

Serve warm or cold with the roti or naan.

Hot chicken ranch dip

SERVES

4–6

1 large boneless, skinless chicken
    breast, approximately 250 g
    (9 oz)
2 bay leaves
5 black peppercorns
2 teaspoons garlic powder
2 teaspoons onion powder
2 teaspoons dried parsley
1 teaspoon dried chives
½ teaspoon salt
½ teaspoon freshly ground
    black pepper
1 small cob loaf
100 g (3½ oz) cream cheese
140 g (5 oz) sour cream
2 tablespoons hot sauce of your
    choice
75 g (2¾ oz) cheddar, grated
75 g (2¾ oz) red Leicester, grated
5–6 chives, chopped, to garnish
corn chips or extra bread, to serve
    (optional)

Put the chicken, bay leaves and black peppercorns in a small saucepan, cover with water and bring to the boil. Reduce the heat and allow to simmer for about 15 minutes, until the chicken is cooked through. Remove the chicken from the water and leave to cool, then shred using two forks.

Mix together the onion and garlic powders, dried herbs and the salt and pepper. Set aside.

Preheat the oven to 180°C (350°F).

To prepare a bread bowl, cut the lid off the cob loaf, then hollow out the inside leaving a 1–1.5 cm (½ in) thick wall.

In a large bowl, mix the cream cheese, sour cream and hot sauce until fully combined. Add the dried mix, three-quarters of the grated cheddar and red Leicester and the chicken, and mix to combine. Spoon the mixture into the bread bowl and top with the remaining grated cheese.

Bake in the oven for 10 minutes, until the cheese has melted. Scatter over the chives and serve with corn chips, extra bread, or just tear into the bowl!

It's a dip, served in a bread bowl you can eat. Can you imagine anything better?

White bean dip with garlic & thyme

SERVES

4

1 small garlic bulb
3 tablespoons olive oil
salt
400 g (14 oz) tinned cannellini
    beans, drained and rinsed
½ teaspoon sumac
5–6 thyme sprigs, leaves picked
juice and zest of ½ lemon
crudités or toasted baguette,
    to serve

Preheat the oven to 200°C (400°F).

Peel off the outermost leaves of the garlic, leaving the bulb intact. Use a sharp knife to slice off the top of the bulb, so that the cut cloves are visible. Place the bulb on a square of foil, then drizzle over 1 tablespoon of the oil and sprinkle with a pinch of salt. Gather up the edges of the foil and scrunch at the top to enclose the garlic in a neat little parcel. Roast in the oven for 40 minutes.

Remove from the oven and leave to cool. Squeeze the garlic out of the individual cloves, discarding the skins, and place in the bowl of a small food processor. Add the beans and remaining ingredients, blitz until smooth.

Serve with the crudités or baguette slices.

Caramelised onion dip

SERVES

4

60 g (2 oz) butter
3 onions, thinly sliced
2 teaspoons salt
2 teaspoons sugar
60 ml (2 fl oz/¼ cup) white wine
300 g (10½ oz) sour cream
225 g (8 oz) cream cheese,
    softened
small handful finely chopped
    parsley
a few dashes of Worcestershire
    sauce or hotsauce
flatbread or crackers, to serve

Heat the butter in a frying pan over medium heat. Add the onion, stir to coat well with the butter and sprinkle with the salt and sugar. Sauté for 10–15 minutes, stirring occasionally. Add half the wine and cook gently for 10 minutes, then add the remaining wine and cook for a further 10–20 minutes, until the onion is soft and deeply golden. Tip the onion onto a cutting board, allow to cool slightly then roughly chop.

In a bowl, combine the cream cheese and sour cream. Mix in the onions and parsley, then taste and season with salt and pepper and a few dashes of sauce. Serve with flatbread or crackers.

This dish is a party classic. If you're in a real hurry or don't want to turn on your stove, you can forego the caramelised onions completely and replace with a packet of French onion soup mix.

A great addition to a light lunch eaten beneath a bougainvillea canopy in a 1000-year-old courtyard in Crete – or on the side of your latenight gyros after a few too many Alphas.

Baked herbed feta

Preheat the oven to 180°C (350°F).

Lay two 30 cm (12 in) squares of foil on top of each other at an angle to make a star shape. Lay a couple of slices of capsicum and onion in the middle of the foil, then plonk the feta on top. Pile the remaining capsicum and onion on top, then finish with the tomato.

Sprinkle over the mint, oregano and chilli, then top with the oregano sprigs, if using. Season with pepper, then drizzle over the olive oil.

Gently gather up the outer edges of the foil. Scrunch the top tightly, so that you have a neat little airtight parcel. Place on a baking tray, ensuring there are no rips in the foil for the delicious juices to escape from. Bake in the oven for 20–25 minutes.

Serve hot in the foil with crusty bread.

Variation

You can amp up the saltiness by adding a handful of kalamata olives or capers.

SERVES

4

1 small red capsicum (bell pepper), thinly sliced
½ red onion, thinly sliced
1 large block of Greek feta, about 200 g (7 oz)
1 large tomato, roughly diced
¼ teaspoon dried mint
¼ teaspoon dried oregano
¼ teaspoon chilli flakes
2 oregano sprigs (optional)
freshly ground black pepper
1 tablespoon olive oil
crusty bread, to serve

Loaded tater tots

SERVES

4

1 kg (2 lb 3 oz) packet of frozen
    tater tots
185 g (6½ oz/1½ cups) grated
    mature cheddar
Guacamole (page 98)
Refried beans (page 99), warmed
sliced pickled jalapeños, to serve
queso fresco or feta, to serve
hot sauce, to serve

Preheat the oven to 210°C (410°F). Place two baking trays in the oven to heat up.

Take the trays out of the oven, and spread the tater tots over the trays. Bake for 10 minutes, then turn them over and bake for another 8–10 minutes, or until crisp. (Alternatively, prepare the tots following the packet instructions.)

Reduce the oven temperature to 170°C (340°F). Spread half the cooked tater tots over the base of a baking dish suitable for serving. Scatter with half the cheddar, then top with the remaining tots and cheddar.

Bake for 5 minutes or until the cheese is melted. Top with the guacamole and refried beans. Scatter with jalapeños and queso fresco, drizzle with hot sauce and serve immediately.

Variation

You can really use whatever you want in this dish – bacon, sliced spring onion (scallions) and sour cream is a great combo. Just cook the tots, top with whatever you like and cover with lots of cheese before baking again.

The best thing about this dish is that it's just as good for the post-drinking hangover as it is with that first beer.

Buffalo wings with blue cheese sauce

SERVES

4

75 g (2¾ oz/½ cup) plain
   (all-purpose) flour
½ teaspoon cayenne pepper
½ teaspoon garlic powder
½ teaspoon salt
1 kg (2 lb 3 oz) chicken wings
185 ml (6 fl oz/¾ cup) melted
   butter
185 ml (6 fl oz/¾ cup) American-
   style hot sauce, such as Crystal,
   Tabasco or Frank's red hot

Blue cheese dip

150 g (5½ oz) blue cheese
250 g (9 oz/1 cup) sour cream
juice of ½ lemon
1 tablespoon white vinegar
salt
freshly ground black pepper

Preheat the oven to 180°C (350°F).

Combine the flour, cayenne pepper, garlic powder and salt in a dish that will comfortably fit the chicken wings. Add the chicken and toss to coat well. Cover with plastic wrap and refrigerate for at least 1 hour.

Whisk together the melted butter and hot sauce. Reserve about a third of the mixture and set aside. Dip the wings in the butter mixture, then place on a baking tray.

Place the wings in the oven. Cook, turning halfway, for 35–40 minutes until caramelised and cooked through.

To make the blue cheese dip, mash the cheese to a paste using a fork, then combine with the sour cream, lemon and vinegar in a small bowl. Taste and season with salt and pepper.

Toss the hot wings in the reserved butter mixture, pile onto a platter and serve with the dip.

Can there be anything better suited to beer drinking than a dish that was literally invented in a bar? Created at the Anchor Bar, buffalo wings are so-named for their hometown of Buffalo, New York.

Fiery lemongrass chicken wings

SERVES

4

1 kg (2 lb 3 oz) chicken wings
7 g (¼ oz/¼ cup) coriander
   (cilantro) leaves
1 bird's eye chilli, thinly sliced

Marinade

2 lemongrass stalks, white part
   only, finely chopped
2 bird's eye chillies, thinly sliced
4 coriander (cilantro) roots
   and stalks, washed and
   finely chopped
4 garlic cloves, finely chopped
2 tablespoons soft brown sugar
1 teaspoon ground turmeric
2 tablespoons peanut oil
juice of 2 limes
2 tablespoons soy sauce
60 ml (2 fl oz/¼ cup) fish sauce

To make the marinade, pound the lemongrass, chilli, coriander and garlic to a paste using a mortar and pestle. Add the sugar and turmeric and mix well. Add the peanut oil, lime juice and sauces and stir to combine.

Transfer the marinade to a dish that will comfortably fit the chicken wings. Add the chicken and coat well. Cover with plastic wrap and refrigerate for at least 2 hours or overnight.

Preheat the oven to 180°C (350°F). Line a baking tray with baking paper.

Place the chicken wings on the prepared tray and place in the oven. Cook, turning halfway through, for 35–40 minutes, until the marinade has caramelised and charred and the chicken is cooked through.

Pile the wings on a platter and garnish with the coriander leaves and sliced chilli.

Front left: Fiery lemongrass chicken
wings (page 123); right: Buffalo wings
with blue cheese dip (page 122)

Chana masala

SERVES

4–6

2 tablespoons ghee or peanut oil

1 teaspoon cumin seeds

1 onion, chopped

2 garlic cloves, crushed

2 cm (¾ in) knob of ginger, finely
    grated

1 bird's eye chilli, chopped

1½ teaspoons sweet paprika

1 teaspoon ground coriander

¼ teaspoon ground turmeric

2 large tomatoes, finely chopped

salt

800 g (1 lb 12 oz) tinned chickpeas
    (garbanzo beans), drained

1 teaspoon garam masala

freshly squeezed lemon juice, to
    taste plus extra wedges to serve

coriander (cilantro) leaves, to serve

steamed basmati rice, Roti canai
    (page 140) or Simple naan
    (page 141), to serve

Heat the ghee or oil in a medium saucepan over medium heat. Add the cumin seeds and allow to sizzle for 10 seconds, then add the onion and cook, stirring occasionally, for 5–6 minutes, until starting to brown. Add the garlic, ginger and chilli and cook for 1 minute until fragrant. Add the paprika, coriander and turmeric and cook, stirring, for 2 minutes, or until fragrant. Add the tomato and stir for 1 minute, then add 250 ml (8½ fl oz/1 cup) of water and a good pinch of salt. Bring to the boil, cover, then reduce the heat and simmer for 10 minutes for the flavours to develop.

Add the chickpeas, then bring to the boil again. Reduce the heat, cover and simmer, stirring occasionally, for 20 minutes. Remove the lid and simmer for a further 10–15 minutes, until the sauce is thickened and the spices have mellowed. Add a little more water if the mixture starts to stick to the bottom of the pan or if it's becoming too thick. Remove from the heat and stir in the garam masala and lemon juice to taste. Adjust the seasoning if necessary.

Serve garnished with the coriander, with steamed rice, roti or naan, and with lemon wedges for squeezing over.

Spicy satay chicken skewers

SERVES

4

600 g (1 lb 5 oz) boneless, skinless
　　chicken thighs, cut into 3 cm
　　(1¼ in) strips
bamboo skewers, soaked in
　　cold water
iceberg lettuce leaves, to serve
cucumber slices, to serve
½ fresh pineapple, cut into chunks

Marinade

2 lemongrass stalks, white part
　　only, thinly sliced
2 garlic cloves, roughly chopped
2 teaspoons finely grated palm
　　sugar
1 teaspoon ground coriander
1 teaspoon ground cumin
1 teaspoon ground turmeric
1 tablespoon peanut oil

Peanut sauce

200 g (7 oz/1¼ cups) raw unsalted
　　peanuts
12 dried red chillies, deseeded
2 lemongrass stalks, white part
　　only, finely chopped
3 shallots, finely chopped
2 garlic cloves, finely chopped
1 tablespoon ground coriander
2 teaspoons finely grated palm
　　sugar
60 ml (2 fl oz/¼ cup) peanut oil
1 tablespoon tamarind paste
1 tablespoon kecap manis
125 ml (4 fl oz/½ cup) coconut milk

To make the marinade, pound the lemongrass and garlic into a paste using a mortar and pestle. Add the palm sugar, coriander, cumin, turmeric and oil and mix well.

Transfer the marinade to a bowl, add the chicken and mix well to coat. Cover with plastic wrap and refrigerate for at least 4 hours or overnight.

To make the sauce, preheat the oven to 180°C (350°F). Spread the peanuts on a baking tray and roast for about 5 minutes, until fragrant and lightly golden. Set aside to cool, then finely chop.

Meanwhile, soak the chillies in hot water for 15 minutes. Drain and roughly chop. Place the chilli in a food processor along with the lemongrass, shallots, garlic, coriander, sugar and peanut oil and process to a paste. Heat a medium saucepan over medium heat and add the chilli paste. Cook, stirring continuously, for 5 minutes. Add 500 ml (17 fl oz/2 cups) of water and bring to the boil, then add the tamarind, kecap manis, peanuts and coconut milk. Simmer over low heat for 5 minutes or until thickened.

Preheat a barbecue grill to medium–high and lightly grease with oil.

Thread three or four chicken strips onto each skewer so that the chicken lies fairly flat. Cook on the grill, turning regularly, for 3–4 minutes, until slightly charred and cooked through. (Cooking time will be determined by the thickness of the chicken.)

Arrange the lettuce, cucumber, pineapple and skewers onto plates. Serve with a small bowl of sauce for each person.

Thai chilli-coconut surf & turf skewers

SERVES

4

24 large raw prawns (shrimp),
    peeled, with tails left intact
300 g (10½ oz) rump or sirloin
    steak, trimmed and thinly sliced
bamboo skewers, soaked in
    cold water
oil, for greasing
cucumber slices, to serve
coriander leaves, to serve
lime wedges, to serve

Chilli–coconut marinade

300 ml (10 fl oz) coconut milk
2 lemongrass stems, white part
    only, finely chopped
6 kaffir lime leaves, finely chopped
2 long red chillies, finely chopped
2 teaspoons grated palm sugar
    (jaggery)
zest and juice of 1 lime
2 tablespoons fish sauce
1 tablespoon kecap manis
2 tablespoons peanut oil

To make the marinade, combine the coconut milk, lemongrass, kaffir lime leaves and chilli in a small saucepan over low heat and simmer, uncovered, for 10 minutes. Set aside to cool to room temperature.

Transfer to a food processor along with the palm sugar, lime zest and juice, fish sauce and kecap manis. Process until well blended. With the motor running, add the oil in a thin, steady stream until incorporated.

Divide the marinade between two large bowls. Add the beef and prawns separately to each bowl. Toss well to coat.

Thread the prawns and beef onto separate skewers, threading the prawns lengthways. Cover and refrigerate for 1 hour.

Preheat a barbecue grill to high and lightly grease with oil.

Cook the skewers for 1–2 minutes each side or until just cooked through.

Serve with cucumber, coriander leaves and lime wedges.

Meat on a stick is the perfect drinking food. You can eat it one-handed, leaving your other hand free to wrap around your pint.

Top right: Spicy satay chicken skewers
(page 128); bottom right: Thai chilli-
coconut surf & turf skewers (page 129)

Chip shop curry sauce & chips

SERVES

4–6

20 g (¾ oz) butter

1 tablespoon peanut oil

2 onions, finely chopped

2 garlic cloves, crushed

1 tablespoon tomato paste
(concentrated purée)

2 tablespoons plain (all-purpose)
flour

1 tablespoon curry powder, or to
taste (use a hot curry powder if
you prefer a spicier curry sauce)

1 teaspoon sweet paprika

375 ml (12½ fl oz/1½ cups)
chicken or vegetable stock

½ teaspoon soy sauce

squeeze of lemon juice, to taste

salt, if needed

4–6 serves prepared hot chips
(fries)

vinegar, to serve

Heat the butter and oil in a medium saucepan over low heat. Add the onion and garlic and cook, stirring frequently, for 6–8 minutes, until softened. Add the tomato paste and cook, stirring, for 1 minute, then stir in the flour, curry powder and paprika. Cook, stirring constantly, for 1–2 minutes, until the mixture just starts to stick on the base of the pan.

Remove the pan from the heat and gradually whisk in the stock until smooth. Return the pan to medium heat, bring to the boil, stirring often, then reduce the heat to low and simmer, stirring occasionally, for 8–10 minutes, until thickened.

Blitz with a hand-held blender for a smooth sauce or just blend it a little to leave some texture. Stir in the soy sauce and lemon juice, and season with salt if necessary. Add a little boiling water to thin the consistency if you prefer a thinner sauce.

To serve, sprinkle the hot chips generously with vinegar and spoon over the sauce.

You could eat these chips at the bar in a cosy London pub, but they're best enjoyed straight out of the paper wrapping standing on the street.

Quick chipotle beef nachos

4–6

1 tablespoon vegetable oil

1 onion, chopped

3 tablespoons tomato paste
(concentrated purée)

2 teaspoons ground cumin

2 garlic cloves, crushed

500 g (1 lb 2 oz) minced
(ground) beef

300 g (10½ oz) tinned kidney
beans, drained and rinsed

250 ml (8½ fl oz/1 cup) beer

2 chipotle chillies in adobo sauce,
chopped, plus 2 teaspoons of
the adobo sauce

large handful of coriander
(cilantro), stalks and leaves
chopped separately, plus extra
leaves to serve

salt

freshly ground black pepper

Classic tortilla chips (page 143),
or 250 g (9 oz) store-bought
tortilla chips

250 g (9 oz/2 cups) grated mature
cheddar

shredded lettuce, to serve

200 g (7 oz) cherry tomatoes,
halved

1 avocado, chopped

sour cream, to serve

sliced pickled jalapeños, to serve

Heat the oil in a frying pan over medium–low heat and cook the onion, stirring often, for 5–6 minutes, until softened. Add the tomato paste, cumin and garlic and cook, stirring, for 2 minutes.

Increase the heat to medium–high and add the beef. Cook, stirring, for 6–8 minutes, until the beef changes colour. Stir in the kidney beans, beer, chopped chipotle chillies, adobo sauce and chopped coriander stalks. Bring to the boil, then reduce the heat and simmer, uncovered, for about 15 minutes, or until the liquid is almost evaporated and the mixture has thickened. Stir in the coriander leaves and season to taste with salt and pepper.

Preheat the oven to 170°C (340°F). Spread half the tortilla chips over the base of a baking dish suitable for serving. Scatter with half the cheese and top with a little less than half the beef mixture.

Repeat with a second layer of tortilla chips, most of the cheese (reserve some for the top), the remaining beef and then the remaining cheese.

Bake for 5 minutes, or until the tortilla chips are lightly toasted and the cheese is melted.

Top with the lettuce, tomato, avocado, sour cream and jalapeños. Serve immediately.

Tex-Mex ground beef tacos

SERVES 4

2 tablespoons vegetable oil
500 g (1 lb 2 oz) minced
    (ground) beef
salt
freshly ground black pepper
4 garlic cloves, crushed
1½ tablespoons dried oregano
2 teaspoons ground cumin
2 teaspoons smoked paprika
pinch of chilli flakes
Corn tortillas (page 142), to serve
sour cream, to serve
grated cheese, to serve
shredded iceberg lettuce, to serve
Pico de gallo (page 103), to serve

Heat 1 tablespoon of the oil in a large frying pan over high heat. Add the beef and cook until browned. Transfer the mixture to a bowl and season with salt and pepper.

Add the remaining oil to the pan and fry the garlic, oregano and spices for 1 minute until fragrant. Return the beef to the pan and toss well, then cook for 3–4 minutes.

Assemble your tacos with the tortillas, beef, sour cream, cheese, lettuce and pico de gallo to your liking, then dig in!

While these tacos have very little to do with actual Mexican cuisine, they sure do taste good with Mexican beer.

Pretzels

SERVES

4

375 g (13 oz/2½ cups) plain
  (all-purpose) baker's flour, plus
  extra for dusting
2 teaspoons instant dried yeast
1 teaspoon salt
½ teaspoon mustard powder
pinch of cayenne pepper
250 ml (8½ fl oz/1 cup) warm
  water, plus extra if needed
olive oil, for greasing
70 g (2½ oz/¼ cup) bicarbonate
  of soda (baking soda)
1 tablespoon brown sugar
1 egg
sea salt flakes or pretzel salt
mustard, to serve

Combine the flour, yeast, salt, mustard powder and cayenne pepper in a large bowl. Add the warm water and mix until you have a rough, soft dough (adding a little extra warm water, if required). Cover the bowl with plastic wrap and set aside for 10 minutes.

Turn the dough out onto a lightly floured work surface and knead for 2–3 minutes until smooth. Place in a lightly oiled bowl, cover with plastic wrap and set aside in a warm place for about 1 hour or until doubled in size.

Turn the dough out again onto a lightly floured work surface and divide into eight equal-sized pieces. Working with one piece of dough at a time, roll the dough against the work surface using the palms of your hands, into a long, skinny rope, about 60 cm (24 in) in length. If the dough shrinks back, set it aside to rest while you work on another piece.

To shape the pretzels, lift the ends of one rope of dough towards the top of your work surface to make a 'u' shape and then twist them together. Bring the twisted rope back down over the bottom loop to form a pretzel shape. Adhere lightly to the base of the loop and place on a baking-paper lined baking tray. Repeat with the remaining dough ropes, then cover loosely with plastic wrap and set aside for 20–30 minutes, until slightly risen.

Preheat the oven to 230°C (450°F).

Pour 2 litres (64 fl oz/8 cups) of water into a large wide saucepan and place over high heat. Bring to the boil, then gradually sprinkle in the bicarbonate of soda. It will foam up rapidly, so be careful. Add the sugar and stir to combine. Reduce the heat until the mixture is simmering.

Working in batches of two to three pretzels at a time, carefully add them to the pan and simmer for 30 seconds. Flip the pretzels over and simmer for a further 30 seconds. Scoop the pretzels out with a slotted spoon, drain and return to the prepared tray.

Whisk the egg with 2 tablespoons of water. Brush the pretzels with the egg mixture and sprinkle with salt.

Bake the pretzels for 12–15 minutes, until cooked through and deep brown. Serve with the mustard on the side.

Roti canai

10

450 g (1 lb/3 cups) plain
    (all-purpose) flour, plus extra
    for dusting
1 teaspoon salt
1 egg
vegetable oil

Combine the flour and salt in a large bowl.

Whisk 250 ml (8½ fl oz/1 cup) of water and the egg in a separate bowl, then pour into the flour. Using your hands, mix to form a soft dough, then cover with plastic wrap or a clean tea towel and set aside for 10 minutes.

Turn the dough out onto a floured work surface and knead for 2–3 minutes, to form a soft, elastic dough.

Roll the dough into a cylinder and divide into 10 even-sized pieces. Knead each piece a few times until smooth, then roll into a ball. Place the balls in a shallow baking dish and completely cover with oil. Cover with plastic wrap or a clean tea towel and leave to rest at room temperature for at least 3 hours, or preferably overnight. Rest in the fridge if the weather is warm, but bring to room temperature before cooking.

Oil a clean work surface. Working with one ball of dough at a time, flatten the dough with the palm of your hand. Working from the edge, gently and gradually stretch the dough outwards as far and as thinly as you can, to roughly the thickness of a sheet of paper and 30 cm (12 in) square. It should be quite transparent. You may get a few holes, but this is okay.

Lift one-third of the dough over the remaining two-thirds. Don't be afraid to gently stretch out the edges – they won't stick together. Fold in the short sides in the same manner to end up with a squarish shape. Gently roll the dough with a rolling pin to enlarge the roti slightly – it should be about 17 cm (6¾ in) square. Repeat with the remaining dough.

Heat a heavy-based non-stick frying pan over medium–high heat. Cook the roti, one at a time, for 1½–2 minutes each side, until golden brown. Slide the bread onto a chopping board and carefully ruffle and bunch up the roti so it becomes flaky. Serve warm.

Simple naan

MAKES

6

80 g (2¾ oz/⅓ cup) plain yoghurt
250 ml (8½ fl oz/1 cup) warm water
1½ teaspoons dried instant yeast
450 g (1 lb/3 cups) plain
   (all-purpose) flour, plus extra
   for dusting
1 teaspoon salt
½ teaspoon baking powder
60 ml (2 fl oz/¼ cup) melted ghee,
   plus extra to brush
½ teaspoon nigella seeds

Mix the yoghurt and water in a large bowl. Stir in the yeast, then add the flour, salt, baking powder and ghee. Mix with your hands to form a soft, sticky dough. Cover and set aside for 20 minutes.

Turn the dough out onto a floured work surface and knead for 1–2 minutes, until quite smooth. Cover and set aside in a warm place for 2–3 hours, until nearly doubled in size.

Preheat the oven to 250°C (480°F) – or the hottest your oven will go. Place two baking trays in the oven to heat up.

Gently lift the dough (so as not to squish all the air out) from the bowl and place on a well-floured work surface. Cut the dough into six wedges.

With floured hands, gently pat and stretch each wedge into a 15 cm (6 in) circle, keeping it thin in the centre and thicker around the edge. Gently brush with ghee.

Working in batches, carefully transfer the dough circles to the hot trays, pulling one side outwards or downwards to form the classic naan teardrop shape. Bake for 6–7 minutes, until golden brown in spots and cooked through. Stack on a plate and cover with a clean tea towel to keep warm and to prevent the naan from drying out.

Alternatively, to cook the naan in a frying pan, heat a large non-stick frying pan or heavy-based cast-iron griddle over medium heat. Working with one piece of dough at a time, brush the top with melted ghee, then transfer to the hot pan, ghee side down, stretching the dough into a teardrop shape as you go. Cook for 2–3 minutes, until golden brown in spots, adjusting the heat if necessary. Brush the top with ghee, flip over and cook for a further 30–60 seconds, until golden and cooked through.

Serve immediately brushed with a little more ghee and sprinkled with nigella seeds.

Corn tortillas

MAKES

16

220 g (8 oz/2 cups) masa harina
(see note)
375 ml (12½ fl oz/1½ cups) warm
water, plus extra if needed
2 teaspoons fine sea salt

Place all the ingredients in a large bowl and, using your hands, mix together until a dough forms. It should be pliable, almost like playdough; add a little more water if it's a bit dry.

Knead the dough for 1–2 minutes, then divide into 16 equal portions. Roll into balls, then cover with a clean tea towel and leave to rest for 20–30 minutes.

Place a ball of dough between two pieces of baking paper, then use a rolling pin to roll it out into a 5 cm (2 in) round tortilla. If you have a tortilla press, place a piece of baking paper on the base plate, then the dough ball in the centre, and another piece of baking paper on top. Press the handle down to sandwich and flatten the dough into a tortilla.

Continue rolling or pressing until you have 16 tortillas. Cover with a clean tea towel until ready to cook.

Heat a large flat cast-iron pan or chargrill pan over medium-high heat. Place a tortilla on the ungreased pan. Flip after 10 seconds, cook for about 45–60 seconds, then flip again and cook for a further 35–50 seconds. The tortilla should feel dry, but not stiff or crumbly, and should be lightly changed in colour.

While cooking the remaining tortillas, keep the cooked tortillas warm by stacking them on top of each other and covering them with a clean tea towel.

Serve immediately.

Variations

To make beetroot (beet) or spinach corn tortillas, replace 60 ml (2 fl oz/¼ cup) of the water with fresh beetroot juice or English spinach juice, for a colourful twist.

Masa harina is a traditional Mexican corn flour used to make tortillas. You can find it at health-food stores or specialty delicatessens.

Classic tortilla chips

SERVES

4

vegetable oil, for deep-frying
300 g (10½ oz) good-quality corn
   tortillas (about 15), torn or cut
   into quarters (if you want to
   make your own, see opposite)
salt

Pour some oil into a deep-fryer or large saucepan, to no more than one-third full. Heat the oil to 180°C (350°F).

Deep-fry the tortillas in batches, stirring occasionally with a slotted spoon, for 2–3 minutes, or until golden and crisp, bringing the oil back to temperature between each batch. Remove with a slotted spoon, drain on paper towel and season with salt.

Alternatively, the tortilla chips can be baked. Preheat the oven to 160°C (320°F). Spread the tortilla pieces over several baking trays in a single layer. Bake for 8–10 minutes, until lightly coloured. The tortilla chips will crisp on cooling.

The tortilla chips can be stored in an airtight container for up to 2 days, and refreshed in a 160°C (320°F) oven for 5 minutes if necessary.

Homemade tortilla chips are particularly good for saucy or wetter toppings – they retain their crunch for longer, won't disintegrate if they become soaked with moisture, and their texture becomes pleasingly chewy. The cooking time will vary depending on the type of tortilla used, so a bit of experimentation with timing may be necessary.

Potato chips

SERVES

4

3 large all-purpose potatoes,
    scrubbed
vegetable oil, for deep-frying
salt flakes

Use a mandoline or sharp knife to slice the potatoes into very thin slices. Try to keep the slices an even thickness so they cook evenly.

Rinse the potato under cold water, then place in a bowl and cover with cold water to help remove some of the starch. Leave to soak for 30 minutes.

Drain the potato and lay the slices on a few layers of paper towel or a clean tea towel. Use more paper towel or another clean tea towel to remove as much water from the slices as you can.

Heat the oil in a large saucepan or deep-fryer to 170°C (340°C). Working in batches, add enough slices to form an even layer in the oil and fry for 4–5 minutes, until just golden brown. The chips will continue to cook and colour after they are removed from the oil, so ensure you remove them when they are just shy of the colour you want them to be.

Drain the chips briefly on paper towel, then leave for a few minutes – they will get crispier as they cool. Sprinkle with sea salt.

The chips are best eaten shortly after cooking.

Beetroot chips

SERVES

4

3 beetroot (beets), about 400 g
(14 oz) in total
2 tablespoons olive oil
salt flakes

Preheat the oven to 180°C (350°F). Line two or three baking trays with baking paper.

Wash and scrub the beetroot, cutting off any hairy roots and the top.

Using a mandoline, cut the beetroot into thin slices, 2 mm ($\frac{1}{8}$ in) if possible. You can also use a sharp knife, working slowly to ensure that the slices are of an even thickness. Transfer the beetroot to a bowl and toss with the oil and a generous pinch of salt flakes.

Lay the slices in a single layer across two or three baking trays. Roast in the oven for 15–18 minutes, rotating the trays after 10 minutes. You'll need to watch the chips carefully after about 13 minutes, as they can burn quickly. They'll be ready when they are slightly curled and brown at the edges.

Leave the chips to cool on a wire rack, then serve. They are best eaten shortly after cooking.

Grissini

MAKES

16

360 g (12½ oz) plain (all-purpose) flour, plus extra for dusting
1½ teaspoons salt
1½ teaspoons instant dried yeast
3 teaspoons sugar
125 ml (4½ fl oz/½ cup) warm water
2 tablespoons olive oil
2 teaspoons sesame seeds

Combine the flour, salt and yeast in a bowl.

Mix the sugar and warm water in a bowl, until the sugar has dissolved, then add the oil.

Add the wet ingredients to the dry, mix briefly until the dough comes together, then turn out onto a floured work surface. Knead the dough for 5–7 minutes, until it becomes smooth. Form the dough into a ball, then place in a lightly oiled bowl, cover with plastic wrap and leave in a warm place for 1 hour.

Preheat the oven to 180°C (350°F). Line two baking trays with baking paper.

Cut the dough into two even pieces. Return one half to the bowl, then roll the other half into a long, thin log, incorporating half the sesame seeds into the dough as you roll it. Cut the log into eight even pieces. Using your hands, roll each piece into long, thin 'sticks', about 20–25 cm (8–10 in) long. Place the grissini on one baking tray, a few centimetres (a couple of inches) apart. Cover with plastic wrap. Repeat the process with the remaining dough then leave to prove for another 10 minutes.

Bake the grissini for 10–12 minutes, rotating the trays halfway through cooking.

Variation

Replace the sesame seeds with $\frac{1}{2}$ teaspoon dried rosemary and $\frac{1}{2}$ teaspoon dried oregano.

Index

Smith Street Books

Published in 2019 by Smith Street Books
Melbourne | Australia
smithstreetbooks.com

ISBN: 978-1-925811-17-9

Publisher: Hannah Koelmeyer
Recipe development: Aisling Coughlan, Caroline Griffiths,
    Deb Kaloper, Sue Herold & Jane O'Shannessy
Additional text: Hannah Koelmeyer & Dave Adams
Food photography: Pete Dillon
Additional photography: Shutterstock, Unsplash, Pexels, Pixabay
Stylist: Deb Kaloper
Food preparation: Sebastien Nichols
Design concept: Murray Batten
Design layout: Megan Ellis
Proofreader: Lucy Heaver, Tusk studio

Printed & bound in China by C&C Offset Printing Co., Ltd.

Book 95
10 9 8 7 6 5 4 3 2 1